How to Make Money Publishing Community News Online

Robert Niles

Copyright © 2012 Robert Niles

Published by Niles Online
315 South Sierra Madre Boulevard, Suite C
Pasadena, CA 91107

Theme Park Insider® is a registered trademark of Robert Niles.

All rights reserved. No part of this book may be reproduced in any manner without written permission, except in the case of brief quotations embodied in critical articles and reviews. For more information, contact Niles Online, 315 South Sierra Madre Boulevard, Suite C, Pasadena, CA 91107.

ISBN: 978-0-9838130-2-6

CONTENTS

Acknowledgements	i
Introduction	iii
1. Want to Start a Business? Find an Unmet Need	1
2. The Community Organizing Model for News Publishing	14
3. Learning about Money	27
4. Analyze the Market and Your Competition	43
5. Building Your Action Team	52
6. Action Plan: Your Startup Checklist	60
7. Time to Mobilize: Daily Reporting	82
8. Implement the Action with Presentation Skills	99
9. Evaluate Your Work through Analytics	128
10. Grow Your Business by Repeating the Process	142
Appendix: Statistics Every Writer Should Know	160
About the Author	192

ACKNOWLEGDEMENTS

I would like to thank Vikki Porter of the Knight Digital Media Center at the University of Southern California's Annenberg School for Communication and Journalism for her support over the years, both in reviving OJR.org and in helping to set up the KDMC News Entrepreneur Boot Camps. I also would like to thank Tom O'Malia, Director Emeritus of the Lloyd Greif Center for Entrepreneurial Studies at the University of Southern California's Marshall School of Business, for his leadership and instruction, which inspired me to write my news entrepreneurship curriculum into this book.

I would not be running successful website businesses today without the hard work of my wife, Laurie Niles, the editor of Violinist.com. And neither of us would have any success online without the loyal support and assistance of the thousands of daily visitors to Violinist.com and ThemeParkInsider.com. *They* built these businesses, and we will be forever grateful for the opportunity to serve their communities.

Finally, I would like to thank those pioneers in online newspaper journalism who knew what was happening to our industry back in the 1990s, and who worked hard to change its direction. Unfortunately, most of them were run out of their jobs for suggesting that an obscenely profitable business needed to change. Now, we need to inspire and train a new generation of reporters and publishers to replace those legacy news businesses that have failed, or are failing.

I hope that this book will help to do that.

INTRODUCTION

If you are an auto racing fan, you probably have heard of Roger Penske. Even if you don't care about race cars, you might have seen his bright yellow Penske rental trucks on highways around the United States. Roger Penske is one of America's top entrepreneurs, having built a multi-billion dollar transportation business that sells, rents and races motor vehicles around the nation. My favorite line about Penske comes from one of his former race car drivers, Indianapolis 500 champion Danny Sullivan, who once said,

"When the music stops, Roger *always* has a chair."

That is who you want to be in life, and in business — someone who is always at least one step ahead of the next change, with a chair waiting to hold you, no matter who or what might try to knock you down in this world.

This book is about the news publishing business, in which I've worked for the past two decades. Over that time, I've won some major awards... and also been paid minimum wage, run out of town, had six bosses in one three-year stretch (without changing my job), watched that employer go out of business, been bought out by another employer, and been laid off.

But, like Roger Penske, whenever the music stopped at some job, I *always* had a chair.

Why? Because in 1995, I started publishing my own websites. I didn't start these as vanity projects, just because I liked seeing my name online. I created my websites because I saw them as ways to meet very specific needs in particular communities. Because my sites met those needs, they've earned money that I've been able to turn to when I needed support.

It's not enough just to build a website. To earn a living in publishing today, you need to know how to organize a community — a collection of readers and sponsors who will support your publication and provide the foundation for your business. In this book, I will explain my "community organizing" model for starting and running a publishing business — a model that I believe can help anyone start a profitable online publishing business.

Before the Internet, most news publishers based their business models on scarcity. Many communities had just one newspaper — so if you wanted to place a classified ad to sell some furniture or a car, or to advertise a job or apartment rental, you had one choice. Newspapers didn't need to build communities. Communities came to them because they had few — or even no — other choices for getting news and placing ads.

The Internet blew apart news monopolies, allowing anyone to publish online for very little cost, and most legacy-media news publishers have yet to adapt. That's created enormous opportunities for independent, start-up publishers. While newspapers and magazines chase the fat, pre-Internet profit margins they'll never see again, you can create a publication that provides the sharp, relevant coverage that can attract a sustainable community of readers and sponsors who are looking for a better alternative.

Are you a journalist who's been laid off, or are you worried about that happening to you? Are you a journalism student, wondering where you'll find a full-time job, with so many newspapers and magazines going out of business or laying off staff? Maybe you're not in the publishing business at all — you're just a resident in a community that's losing (or lost) its daily news coverage and who wants to find a way to get back that needed coverage.

The lessons in this book can help anyone to launch and run a publishing business that can meet the information needs of a community, while providing a income that can give you true job security. After all, the only boss you can be certain will never fire you is... *you*.

Don't be naive about what this will require, however. This isn't some get-rich-quick book, or a guide to building "passive income." The days are long over when people could throw up a bunch of static webpages, packed with lucrative "keywords," and watch the search engines send them gobs of traffic and money.

Nor is this a recipe book — a fixed set of specific instructions that anyone can follow to cook up a profitable publishing business. The specific mix of steps needed to build a money-making publication will vary by each unique community covered, and by each unique publisher who sets out to cover it. Any book that tries to sell you on "one true way" to make a business work is selling you out. Publishing today requires work — hard effort and long hours — but if you do it right, finding a need that you love to fulfill, you can *and will* make money online.

I'd recommend that you read through the entire book before starting your publication. You'll want to see the entire roadmap before beginning your trip. However, at the end of each chapter, I've provided an exercise which I hope that you will complete before proceeding to the next chapter. These exercises will prepare you for your journey, and completing them as you read the book will ensure that you have the personal commitment necessary to launch and run an independent business. Along the way, I'll be citing many websites and resources that can help your efforts. To make finding those webpages easier, I've linked them all on my website at *www.robertniles.com/data*.

So let's get started. Let's learn about online publishing — the right way — and discover some of the ways that you can use the power of online publishing to find and fulfill the needs of your community. It's important work, and we need people like you to do it.

Let's get started building your chair.

1 WANT TO START A BUSINESS? FIND AN UNMET NEED

Here's the first question to ask yourself, before you build a website:

"Why would anyone pay me money to do this?"

I've heard plenty of answers to this question — almost all of them wrong. You might think this question too personal to have a "wrong" answer, but people who think that are the ones most likely to come up with a wrong answer.

You see, *no one cares* why you want to start a new business. No one cares about anyone's award-winning-career as a newspaper reporter. No one cares about your heartfelt passion for your hometown. No one cares about the bills you have to pay or your need to find a new way to make some cash.

Get over it. Accept the fact that no one cares about you. But people *do* care about themselves, and if you can meet an unfilled need for people, they will pay you money to do it.

Starting a business — whether it's a news website, an auto

repair shop or an organic grocery store — is all about finding an unmet need in a community and providing a good or service that takes fulfills it. Want to start a business? Then start by looking for the need in a community.

This is the only acceptable answer to the question I asked above. Your answer to the question, "Why would anyone pay me money to do this?" must be: "Because I will meet a need no one else can."

Now, what is that need? And how will you meet it? Those are the personal questions you will need to answer as an individual. But never forget that the core concept behind any successful publication is always the same: it meets a need for its customers. Keep your focus on that core concept and you'll have a chance at success in publishing.

Ultimately, you will be in the business of helping your customers. Plenty of people have started websites for selfish reasons — heck, I've done it a few times, too. But the people who have succeeded in making those websites into profitable businesses have found ways to meet the needs of paying customers along the way. The sooner you change your focus as a publisher to customer service, the sooner you'll be earning the income that can transform your publication into a sustainable business.

Who is your customer?

If your mission is to serve a customer, you first must know whom that customer is. Too many publishers fail to identify their customers. So who is your customer? Here's the easy answer, taught to me by Tom O'Malia, Director Emeritus of the Lloyd Greif Center for Entrepreneurial Studies at the University of Southern California's Marshall School of Business:

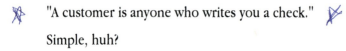
"A customer is anyone who writes you a check."

Simple, huh?

Yet it's depressing to see how many publishers fail to understand that. Too many online publishers think that their customers are the readers clicking around online — people who never pay them a dime. Too many newspaper publishers think their customers are home delivery readers, whose subscription fees hardly cover the cost of printing and delivery — forget about the cost of reporting and producing the paper.

Unless they're collectively paying you enough to cover a significant portion of the cost of doing business, those readers are not your customers. They're your *audience*, instead.

Audience is important. Without an audience, you've got no chance of landing paying customers. Serving an audience therefore will be an important part of your publishing business. But for most news publications, the audience is *not* the customer. So, then, who is?

Now, if you are a current news reporter or a journalism student, don't stop reading after the next paragraph, okay? This will all work out fine, just stick with me for a few more paragraphs. (And if you're not a journalism veteran, just ignore this paragraph. You probably aren't coming to this book with the news industry's philosophical baggage — which teaches that thinking about money is bad and which prevents many news reporters from becoming successful publishers. Be thankful for that.)

Remember, the customer is "anyone who writes you a check." So for most news publishers, your customer is... your advertisers. If you're going to succeed publishing an ad-supported publication, you've got to meet the needs of your advertisers.

Unfortunately, decades of ethics training in the journalism industry have taught news reporters not only that they should ignore the needs of their publication's advertisers, but that doing anything to help an advertiser constitutes an egregious violation of professional ethics. So when I write that a publisher's primary responsibility as a business person is to meet the needs of his or her customers (in other words, advertisers), I suspect many news reporters will want to quit reading, abandon their dreams of becoming a publisher and look for another way to make money instead.

But whom would that help? Not communities that need more and better coverage. Not the business owners who need simpler, more direct ways of connecting with their local community than trying to get noticed through Google. Giving up on your dream of community publishing really only helps existing news publishers, who will have one fewer competitor to face.

Journalism leaders originally developed these ethical principles to ensure that reporters didn't end up writing glorified ads for sponsors, instead of reporting accurate news stories. The idea was to prevent writers from putting the needs of advertisers over the needs of the audience.

But journalism ethics fail if they discourage new publishers from getting into the business. In this book, I will argue that you can serve both your readers and your customers. That's because the best way to meet the needs of advertisers *is* to serve the needs of your audience. Businesses have a huge need to connect with people who aren't yet *their* customers. They need to reach an audience of people who might likely be interested in their business, but who haven't been motivated enough to walk in (or click over) and buy anything yet. Publishers meet that need by selling access to *their* audience, through advertising.

So if you don't have an audience that advertisers want to reach, you can't meet the needs of those advertisers.

Your challenge, as a publisher, is to meet the needs of an audience so that enough of them read your publication to make it an attractive channel through which to meet the needs of your customers (advertisers). You can do both, *and you must*.

Thinking about going the non-profit route, to avoid that whole icky advertiser thing? Keep this in mind, then: As digital entrepreneur and journalist Tom Davidson said at a Knight Digital Media Center boot camp, "Non-profit isn't a business model. It's a tax status." The core principle behind the business remains the same. Instead of getting money from advertisers trying to reach your audience, you'll be soliciting money from foundations and other organizations trying to reach your audience. You're still selling access to your audience, either way. Plus, you'll need to deal with reams of tax forms and regulations that many for-profit publishers can ignore.

What about direct sales, some would-be publishers might ask? Why not start a publication that readers pay for directly, so that you don't have to worry yourself with meeting the needs of advertisers or foundations?

People are paying publishers billions of dollars a year to read a class of publications that has no advertising or foundation support. These publications are books, and smart news publishers are taking advantage of a revolution in eBook publishing to cash in with them. I'll write more about eBook publishing later, and I'll make an argument for why they should become an important part of your publishing strategy.

But even with eBooks, you won't make many sales if you don't build an audience first. So before we think any more about customers, let's start with our audience and finding a need you can address that will build an audience large enough to become commercially viable — no matter whom your customers turn out to be.

Who is your audience, and what do they need?

Let's start thinking about the community you wish to cover. It doesn't have to be a physical, geographic community. Some of the most successful individually-published news sites on the Internet are niche-topic sites with a global readership. Remember that, online, you don't have to pay to print and ship copies of your publication to readers. It's just as inexpensive to serve a reader in a different hemisphere as it is to serve one down the street. You don't need to limit your focus by geography.

At the same time, because you don't have to pay the costs of expensive printing and distribution networks, you can operate a news website for very low cost. So low, in fact, that you could limit your focus to a very small geographic community and still earn enough revenue to stay in business. That's the "hyperlocal," or neighborhood, model of online news publishing. If you do it right, your neighborhood could have a commercially successful publication of its own, with more coverage, in greater depth, than any metropolitan daily ever provided it.

Whether you choose a niche-topic community or a geographic community to serve with your publication, you'll need to identify some ongoing need within that community that your publication will meet. With all the media options consumers have today — thousands of television channels, millions of websites and eBooks, social media, games — your publication had better reward its readers with something of significant value if you are to have any hope of building an audience. If you don't alleviate some pain or unmet need in the lives of people in your community, these people will ignore you in favor of other media options that do deliver value in return for their time and attention.

So what can you do to help people in your chosen community?

To help focus your answer to that question, consider what Tom O'Malia calls the "four whys":

- Why is this important?
- Why is now the time to do this?
- Why are you the one who can do this?
- Why have you come to me?

Imagine yourself talking with a potential reader of your new publication. You have 15 seconds to convince this person to become a reader of your website. In crafting your "pitch" to this potential reader, imagine that he or she has asked you these four questions, which you'll need to answer in your pitch.

The first question addresses the need: What are you going to do with your website, and why is it important to the potential reader? The second question gets at why this is a real, immediate *pain* that simply must be addressed now. (That is what makes your site valuable, not just to its readers, but also to the sponsors and backers you'll eventually approach for financial support.) The third question gives you the opportunity to sell readers on *your* solution to their problem — to tell them why you, alone, have the knowledge, insight and ability to deliver the solution you've offered. Finally, the fourth question allows you to make an individual connection with this potential reader and to deliver a personal invitation to join your publication's readership community.

Did I mention you've got 15 seconds to deliver this pitch? Maybe less, depending upon the attention span of the person listening. Business-school types call this the "elevator pitch" because it's designed to be delivered in the time an elevator takes to get from one floor to another, when your audience is captive and can't go anywhere to get away from you.

Business school students practice elevator pitches to convince investors to buy into a start-up company. But the elevator pitch is an essential skill for publishers, too. You might not be asking people to buy stock in your publication, but you are asking them to give up something just as valuable: their time. That is, the time to read your website on a regular basis. That's a precious asset, and you should respect it enough to deliver real value to your readers in return.

As you think about audiences you might serve, and how you might serve them, ask yourself if what you will deliver for this audience is so clear, and so urgently needed, that you can describe it in a convincing 15-second pitch. If the idea for your website is too complex to explain in that short time, then you'll need to keep thinking. Find a concept that can resonate immediately with potential readers.

Look for an ongoing need. If you want to build a business that will provide a good living for years to come, you won't want to choose to address a need that can be eliminated permanently for everyone in just a few weeks or months. Instead address something more fundamental than the immediate, temporary issues that pop up from time to time in everyone's lives.

Don't cop out by saying you'll alleviate your audience's need "for information." People are drowning in information. They don't need more. If they have any need for information, it's for better and more focused news. Dig deeper. What specific information does your audience need? *Why* does it needs that information? For what reasons are your potential readers using information? What is it doing for them? *That* gets at the needs and pains in your readers' lives. When you start thinking about how and why people use information in their lives — whether it be information on schools, food, jobs, community businesses, questions of faith — then you are on the path to finding the specific needs that your publication can meet.

Two examples of finding, and addressing, audience and customer needs

I help publish two niche-topic websites: ThemeParkInsider.com and Violinist.com. As you probably can guess from the domain names, these sites cover theme parks and the violin, respectively. I started the first site because I was a former Walt Disney World employee and lifelong theme park fan who liked talking about parks with other fans online. I started the second when I bought the domain name for my wife, a professional violinist, as a geeky Christmas present.

But the sites grew into viable businesses because each met at least one need for both its readers and its eventual advertisers. In fact, they each addressed multiple needs.

ThemeParkInsider.com addresses the fear people have that they won't get their money's worth on vacation. It serves families planning what can be very expensive vacations to popular theme park resorts around the world — Walt Disney World and Universal Orlando in Florida, Disneyland in California, and other Disney, Universal and SeaWorld theme parks in United States, France, Japan and Singapore. If you're going to drop several thousand dollars on a theme park vacation, you want to make sure that you and your family are going to have the best possible time in return for spending all that money. ThemeParkInsider.com "crowdsources" theme park vacation planning, providing reader ratings, reviews and comments from thousands of other vacationers, to help readers plan a vacation their families will enjoy.

In 1999, when I started the website that would become ThemeParkInsider.com, very few sites were providing forums for reader ratings and reviews of anything. The rare theme park coverage in daily newspapers tended to be fluffy pieces, often written by freelancers who accepted free trips as part of their "research." By providing the real-world experiences of consumers who paid their own way into the parks, my site provided a more accurate, honest and detailed perspective than other media reports on theme parks.

Over time, plenty of other sites started doing pretty much the same thing for all aspects of travel. Today, you can find reader reviews on sites such as Yelp, TripAdvisor, Hotels.com and more. If I'd never adjusted what I offer on ThemeParkInsider.com, the site could have lost its audience as its readers switched to more comprehensive rating-and-review websites elsewhere.

So I made two major changes to the site in response. First, I added news coverage by blogging about theme parks on a daily basis. That appealed to fans who didn't want to leave behind the joy of their vacations when they returned home. They could relive the fun by reading more about their favorite parks and keeping engaged with other theme park fans. They also could learn about new developments and attractions around the world, helping them to plan future trips.

Second, I decided to make my site's narrow focus a strength, rather than a weakness. Knowing I couldn't keep up with Yelp and TripAdvisor, I decided to scale back instead of expand. We stopped trying to cover every theme and amusement park in the world, focusing instead just on the most popular theme parks — especially those from Disney, Universal and SeaWorld Parks & Entertainment. If we couldn't cover everything, we'd be the smartest specialists about what we did cover. This move also helped position us between Disney-fan sites that covered Disney World and Disneyland but gave only scant attention to other theme parks, and roller-coaster-fan sites that covered hundreds of amusement parks around the world, but paid little attention to attractions other than roller coasters.

As it turns out, with that decision, ThemeParkInsider.com started focusing on the most lucrative audience in the theme park business — people planning multi-day visits to top-end theme park resorts, but who didn't already have unbreakable brand loyalty to market-leader Disney. By doing that, we addressed the advertisers' need — their need to focus exclusively on visitors willing to spend for a week-long theme park resort vacation, but who weren't already locked into Disney. Obviously, these are the people Universal and SeaWorld (and the hotels located near them) want to reach. But they also are the people Disney targets as well, as it looks to expand its market beyond its existing fans.

On Violinist.com, which started in 1996, we provided something that never had been widely available before — daily news, features, insight and instruction from violinists around the world. Classical music coverage in pre-Internet media was published infrequently and typically written by critics who'd never performed music on a professional level. While many of them were quite knowledgeable about music, the need to write for a general audience forced them to write pieces that simply lacked the detail and professional insight that student and professional violinists wanted from classical music coverage.

A few print magazines targeted violinists, but they came out only once a month or less, and lacked the interactivity we could offer as a website. We addressed violinists' need for a global forum in which to come together, self-identify, share experiences and learn from one another — and to do so on a daily basis. By building that violin community through our website, we created an opportunity for advertisers to reach violinists on a more frequent basis than ever before. Publishing online instead of in print, we could offer lower advertising rates than the magazines, as well as the opportunity to reach a younger, less brand-loyal audience that never started reading about the violin in print.

In both cases, we began by targeting an audience need, and by doing that, we built an audience that helped us offer advertisers the opportunity to address *their* needs as well.

Also in both cases, we built our audiences with intent: not simply trying to attract every potential reader we could, but trying to tailor our editorial content and technical functionality to attract a specific set of readers — the readers certain advertisers were most trying to reach and couldn't get to through any other single source than us.

In envisioning your audience, then, focus your efforts not just to attract readers, but to attract readers that will, in turn, attract financial backers for your site, whether they be advertisers or non-profit foundations with their own needs and agendas. Getting the focus right up front will save you an immense amount of time and effort later, when you begin to approach potential backers and seek financial support for your publication.

EXERCISE

Throughout the book, I'll be offering exercises to help you toward becoming a successful publisher. The sooner you get into the habit of doing the things you need to do to succeed as a publisher, the sooner you will achieve that success. So, please, don't skip these assignments. Put down the book for as long as it takes to complete them, before proceeding. You'll thank yourself in the end, if you make that effort.

Keep all your assignment work in one place — either in a folder on your computer, or in a bound-paper journal, if you're old-school about written assignments. You'll want to be able to see your work as you proceed on your journey toward launching your business.

Your first assignment? Craft a 15-second pitch that will convince a potential reader to visit your new website. In it, be sure to answer Tom O'Malia's "four whys." And try to craft a pitch that will be especially enticing to a reader who fits the audience you believe will be most attractive to financial supporters. In other words, if you're building a website about West Shelbyville, it's okay if someone from East Springfield who hears your pitch says, "meh," and never visits. Your backers want to reach people in West Shelbyville, after all.

Write your pitch, memorize it, then test the pitch on at

least four people (no more than one family member). Revise as you see fit. Keep refining your pitch, because you'll need it as long as you're in the publishing business.

2 THE COMMUNITY ORGANIZING MODEL FOR NEWS PUBLISHING

In past generations, being in the news business required buying an expensive printing press or convincing the government to award you a hard-to-get broadcasting license. The hassle and expense of getting those kept most would-be publishers out of the market... which worked very well for people who did get through. Once you had a printing press or a broadcast license, you were golden. No one else was likely to come along to compete with you. The high barrier to entry in the publishing business kept the number of publishers relatively low, limiting the supply of information, which made what information was available more valuable to the public. Pretty sweet deal, huh? So long as no one ever invented a cheaper way to publish, or an easier way to broadcast, publishers could keep charging advertisers whatever they wanted, making fat profits forever.

The Internet, of course, blew up that model for the news industry. Today, anyone with an Internet connection can publish for free, through services such as Blogger, Tumblr and YouTube. That's created an enormous number of new competitors for newspapers and television stations, and an enormous number of new publications where advertisers can place their ads. Longtime publishers have had to slash the prices they charge advertisers, and they're still losing customers, driving newspaper advertising revenue down to its lowest levels in 60 years.

But I don't want you to think about the newspaper industry. Or television stations. Focus, as always, on your audience and your customers. Think about *their* needs, their pains and how the Internet publishing revolution has affected them.

The old problem — back in the days when we had one newspaper and three-to-five TV stations in most cities — was a lack of information, or a lack of advertising options. Today — with millions of websites, podcasts and video blogs — the problem is often *too much* information, or *too many* advertising choices. You can't win an audience just by showing up, the way you could by publishing a newspaper or starting a TV station 40 years ago. Heck, by giving people one more information option, you're *adding* to people's pain.

So even if you believe you've identified the most urgent need felt by your potential audience and customers, none of them is going to come looking for you to let you address that. They're likely overwhelmed by existing information sources and in no mood to seek another one. You're going to have to work aggressively to build your audience and your customer base — far more aggressively than publishers have had to do in the past. You are going to have to work to build the virtual community you wish to serve.

Fortunately, others have developed proven methods to build and motivate communities of interested people. Political activists have developed a multi-step process of "community organizing" that works not only for getting people involved in political campaigns and community projects, but also for building online communities.

I learned about community organizing studying political

science and watching countless election campaigns. I first wrote about community organizing for the publishing business in a 2010 blog post for OJR.org: "Doing Journalism in 2010 is an Act of Community Organizing."
<http://www.ojr.org/ojr/people/robert/201001/1810> And I've described these community organizing principles in classes I've taught for the Knight Digital Media Center's News Entrepreneur Boot Camps at the University of Southern California.

Community organizing is a seven-step process, and you can use these same steps to help you build the audience base that will, in turn, attract customers to your new publishing business. They are common-sense steps that build upon each other in moving you forward to attract, retain and expand the community you wish to serve. Even after you've launched your business, you can continue to use these principles to maintain and expand your business. They provide an evergreen roadmap that will help guide any business owner to work better with the public she or he serves.

We will be talking about these seven steps for the rest of this book. Every stage in building, launching and running a business reflects one of these seven steps. We've already started with the first.

Step 1: Assessing the community

Remember when I asked you to "find a need"? That was step one in community organizing: assessing the community.

You'd have to be pretty arrogant to believe you could organize a community without first getting to know it. So do. Even if you've lived in a particular community your entire life and think you know it well, take this opportunity to examine it from other perspectives. Challenge your assumptions. Go to church and community meetings you wouldn't typically attend. Hang out in the coffeehouse on the other side of town. Lurk in community forums online. Call or email people you've seen in the news and ask to meet them for coffee or lunch. Find out what they think the needs in the community are.

You don't have to do what any of these people tell you, but you should get to know their perspectives.

Once you've found what you believe to be the most pressing needs in the community, you should continue to assess them with some formal tests. In Chapter 4, we'll look at Tom O'Malia's "feasibility funnel" for testing a new business idea. We'll also ask you to find and list potential competitors to your publication, along with estimates of their incomes and expenses. To do that, you'll need to take a hard look at other publications serving the market. You'll need to look at other media that people in the community use to communicate, as well. Think that the church newsletter and local PTA discussion board aren't competitors? If they provide ways that people report and share news in the community, they could be.

In assessing the community, you'll need to assess your role within it, too. Remember the "four whys"? One of those was "Why are you the one who can do this?" When you first approach people to become part of your project — whether as readers, participants, advertisers or financial supporters — all you'll have to offer them is... you.

What will you offer them — in personal experience, knowledge, outlook and enthusiasm — that will convince them to give their time, attention, effort and money to your business? Why are you the one who can do this? If you don't know how you fit within your community — what unique skills and talents you bring to it — you're not going to be able to raise the support you will need to launch your business and make it a success.

Step 2: Creating an action team

Yes, you will need support. No one on Earth ever has built a business by himself.

In 2001, ThemeParkInsider.com won an Online Journalism Award from the Columbia Graduate School of Journalism and the Online News Association for our coverage of injury accidents at theme parks around the United States. At the time, I got quite a bit of publicity for being the first "one-person website" to win a major journalism award. But even though I didn't have any employees or paid staff working with me on ThemeParkInsider.com, I didn't build that site, or that award-winning project, by myself. Hundreds of ThemeParkInsider.com readers and volunteers contributed accident reports that allowed us to build that accident database. Without that action team, there would be no accident project, no award and no website. (I'll write about more in Chapter 10 about the development of this project.)

You will need an action team to help you bring your publication business from idea to money-making reality. Start with your family. Building a business will disrupt whatever routine you've developed in your daily life. Whether you're starting a business on the side while you continue to work elsewhere, or you're diving into this effort full-time from the start, you're going to need to spend many hours on this business that you'd previously spent doing something else. As you're trying to build new relationships with your community and potential business partners, please don't let that effort damage or destroy your existing relationships with your family. Find ways to get their support — ideally, by finding ways to get them involved in the project. This new business will change your relationship with the people closest to you. It's up to you to determine whether your business will strengthen — or strain — your relationships with your family.

In 1996, I bought by wife the domain Violinist.com as a gag Christmas present. At the time, she had only the vaguest idea of what an Internet domain was. But as I built ThemeParkInsider.com in the evenings over the years that I worked at various newspapers, she had a domain to play with, too. By getting her active with a website covering the topic she most cared about, she could better understand what I was doing with *my* website, even though it covered another topic. And when the time came to make our websites a full-time job, she had a domain that she could edit as well. Family members alone won't be enough, though. You'll need to create additional relationships to develop a fully-powered action team.

Take the next step by finding a mentor — a successful entrepreneur outside your family or current circle of friends and colleagues with whom you can talk about what you're trying to do, and who will share her or his story with you. As new and different as starting a business might feel to you, plenty of people have done this before. Learn what you can from them to minimize mistakes and maximize opportunities as you go forward.

Step 3: Developing an action plan

Once you've assessed the community and started building relationships, then it will be time to start making plans. In Chapter 6, I'll present a checklist to guide you through the processes of setting up a website, as well as setting up a formal business entity to run it. Even if you are working by yourself, you'll need to create some formal legal structure for your business, to help you cash checks and comply with local laws and regulations regarding the running of a business.

But those checklists just get you started. Remember, this step is *developing* an action plan, not just using someone else's. This is the step where you "connect the dots" between the skills and talents of you and your action team and the needs of the community you've chosen to serve. How are you going to apply the potential of what you and your team can do to what the readers, advertisers and funders in your community need done?

Obviously, to run a website publishing business you will need to set up a website. We'll provide you some basic action steps for doing that in Chapter 6. But you'll need to fill that new website with plenty of engaging articles and other content and services to attract an audience and customers. How often will you publish? What types of articles will you include? Who will write them? Are you going to include photos, video, audio or reader feedback in your posts? How's that going to happen? Your initial attempts to answer those and many other questions will become part of your action plan.

Blogging tools have made Internet publishing so easy that you don't really need an action plan to put content online. Just type whatever comes to mind and go. But that's rarely the best way to serve an audience. You'll grow your audience much larger and more quickly if you offer them some consistency. Set a regular publishing schedule. Come up with recurring features that readers can come to expect from you on certain times on certain days. You want to make coming to your publication a habit, and the best way to do that for your readers is to establish some regular habits for yourself.

The freedom from form that the Internet offers you can be a wonderful, liberating asset for your publishing business. But if you're not careful, it can lull you into sloppy planning and thoughtless, formless publishing that leaves readers cold, never to return to your site. Publish with intent, always thinking about what you're putting up there for the public to read and to experience. Develop an action plan before you go public with your work.

Step 4: Mobilizing to action

Okay, you've got your team and your plan. It's time to get going, right?

Not so fast.

I told this story to my children just before they first took the big standardized tests that the state makes all public school students take each year: A teacher hands out a test to all of her students. On the top of the page, the test's instructions say: "Please read through all the questions before answering any of them." So the good student starts reading the questions and is horrified. The test starts with simple questions — basic addition problems and easy vocabulary questions. But then it gets hard. Really hard. The test asks long essay questions as well as math problems using complex equations with symbols the student's never seen. Then the test asks the student to do science experiments — difficult ones, with chemicals and small lab animals the school might not even have. Finally, the student gets to the last question: "Now that you've read all the questions, as you were asked to do first, simply write your name at the top of the test sheet and put down your pencil. Ignore all the other questions on the test." The student does so, then spends the rest of the class period laughing quietly to herself as her classmates who didn't pay attention to the instructions scream and swear in frustration.

Mobilizing to action is where you take a moment to read the instructions before diving into the test. It's where you have that pre-game meeting with your action team, to talk about what you're about to do and make sure you're all playing with the same game plan. Mobilizing to action allows you to ensure that your action team is in place and your action plan solid before you launch, when a misstep can permanently damage your relationship with readers and advertisers.

Journalists can think of "mobilizing to action" like this: It's the reporting you do before you write the story. Or the editorial meeting you have before you lay out the paper's front page. If you've ever worked in sales, think of this step as the social networking you do with a potential client before you jump into your sales pitch.

Sometimes, this step leads you to return to Step 2 or Step 3 before you move on. Maybe an action team member bails on you. Maybe you discover something you missed in your plan. Or perhaps the conversations with your team (or even with yourself) reveal an opportunity you'd missed.

Step 5: Implementing the action

You've gotten to know the community you want to serve, built a team and a plan for serving it, and talked about what you're going to do. Now it's time to do it. Whether it is launching your website, publishing your book, posting your article, selling an ad or hosting an event, implementing the action comes only after you've worked on building the foundation necessary to support the project.

In Chapter 8, we'll address some of the many ways that publishers implement the action. We'll offer tips for effective online writing, community management, public speaking, video production and eBook publishing. No matter which action you choose, the work you do to understand whom you are serving — and their needs — will help ensure that your action pays off with a strong return on that investment of time and effort.

Step 6: Evaluating what you've done

How will you measure the return on your investment? That's Step 6 in our community organizing model for news publishing. Smart publishers use a variety of data to measure how many people are reading and responding to their work, who's spreading it around the Internet, what's bringing people into the website, and which ads are getting the most response.

Ultimately, only one measurement matters in business: money. In Chapter 9, we'll look at the metrics publishers use to evaluate their business, including the bottom line. But remember this — don't judge specific, individual steps you take by how much money they make for you. In more than a decade of publishing, I've never put up an article that made enough money on its own to pay for itself on its first day after publication. Many posts *never* earn enough ad revenue from their individual page alone to pay for the expense of reporting and writing them. If I only wrote pieces that I could justify using strict cost/revenue accounting, I'd never post anything on my website.

Obviously, an empty website's not going to earn much money, either.

How can metrics help you run a successful business? Use them in context with other metrics — never look at individual metrics alone. When I was in graduate school, I worked checking groceries for a few weeks before joining the staff at the local newspaper. Every week, the store owner would put some item on sale for less than it cost him to stock the item. Maybe it'd be a gallon of milk for a couple bucks. Or a buy-one, get-one-free offer on breakfast cereal. He'd feature the deal in his weekly ad in the local paper and on big signs painted on the front window of the store.

The owner told us that these deals were his "loss leader" for the week. He knew he'd lose money on every sale of these items, but he also knew that almost no one would come into his store to buy only the item on sale. They'd walk the aisles and pick up several other things they'd need as well. The profit on those items would more than cover the loss on the sale product. The "loss leader" was there to bring people into his store, luring them from the other grocery in town.

Original reporting for blog posts and news articles is the loss leader of the news industry. These pieces cost money to produce — more than they'll earn back on ad revenue from those individual pages on the day they're published. But you need them to build a large and loyal audience of readers who will not only come to your website for those pieces, but also stick around and click around, reading other pages and participating in comments and discussion forums. While those original articles might not make much money on their own, they'll drive that the traffic that, *in aggregate*, can help make your publication profitable. The value of the Web is not in the individual strands. It's in the web that connects them.

On my websites, we make the majority of our ad revenue on our home pages and on sharply-focused discussion post pages. But those pages would have little or no traffic if it weren't for the stories and blog posts that draw the bulk of our readers to the site.

Learn to use your metrics to help you identify things such as effective "loss leaders" that help increase revenue across the site. Don't fall into the trap of misusing metrics. Don't be like those newspaper publishers who start firing their reporters because they don't earn their way on their own.

Step 7: Repeat

Communities grow, contract, advance and evolve. The effort to organize communities never ends. Something's always changing. That's great for news publishers — they're always something new to cover. But it also means that you'll forever be repeating this community organizing process, every day that you work as a publisher.

Perhaps it's simply to report and write the day's blog posts. Or maybe you'll take on more ambitious tasks, such as editing your first eBook or promoting your first offline meeting for website readers. No matter what task you choose, you should use these same seven steps to approach your project: Get to know your target. Build a team. Make a plan. Talk about it. Implement it. See how you did. Then go back and do it again, until you get it right. Once you do, keep doing it, and add another project to the mix.

Everyone I know who has earned success in independent online publishing has been able to move away from thinking like an employee, who looks for a single source of income to support himself or herself. Instead, these people think like entrepreneurs — always looking for new projects, new sources of income to add to the mix that, collectively, bring in enough cash to keep them afloat.

In the news business, many successful freelancers long have

worked this way, always trying to have enough projects going to bring in an adequate income (or more!) Bring that attitude toward publishing. Don't settle for landing a single donor, advertiser or sugar daddy to pay your way. That leaves you as dependent as a newsroom employee, living in dread of the next round of layoffs. You'll only achieve financial independence in your publishing business if you diversify your income, using the community organizing principles to develop a variety of projects, with a variety of customers, that collectively will keep bring in enough money to keep you moving forward, even as individual projects and customers fall away, as some inevitably will.

> **EXERCISE**
>
> Talk to at least three business owners or managers in your community. (These should be people who have the authority to spend money on their businesses' behalf, without having to get approval from a boss.) Ask them what they see as the number-one unmet need for their business or the community they serve. Then ask what they'd be willing to pay if someone met that need. These don't have to be needs that you'd meet with your publishing business. You're trying to get a sense for what local businesses leaders (the type of people most likely to become your customers) see as the big needs in the community, and what price they'd put on meeting those needs.
>
> Were these the same community needs you saw? Think about how you can improve your ability to recognize business opportunities in your chosen community.

3 LEARNING ABOUT MONEY

Let's face it. For most people, life's rough without money. That's why money causes more stress for more people than just about anything else in life. The fear of not of having money keeps an uncounted number of people working in jobs they hate, for people they can't stand. When I work with people who are trying to start their own publishing businesses, their number-one question always is the same: How am I going to make money?

So let's learn about money in the publishing business before we bring up anything else in this book. In this chapter, I'll describe several of the ways that news publishers are earning money online, and I'll introduce the vocabulary that online publishers use to talk about money. And don't forget that income is only half the issue with money. We'll also talk about expenses and how keeping your expenses down often provides your best path to making a profit in a competitive market.

But before we begin, let's get to the big secret — the secret that every successful business person has learned about income. It's the lesson you will need to learn if you're to earn enough income to make your business successful, too. Here's the secret to making money:

Don't worry about making money.

Of course, hearing that is maddeningly frustrating for someone who's just starting out, with bills to pay and no income. But the truth is that if you take care of building and cultivating a community — if you find and meet a community need — the money will come looking for you. Violin shops came to us asking to buy ads on Violinist.com long before it occurred to us that we might be able to sell ads on the site. They recognized the value that our site was creating *for them* by expanding and cultivating a market for the violin. One early advertiser told us that he wanted to make sure that we weren't running the site as a hobby, to be dropped and closed when we grew tired of it. He said that he considered the community we had built so important that he wanted to make sure that we were earning enough income from it that we'd be certain to keep it going.

That is where you want to get with your publishing business.

Former Disneyland President Jack Lindquist once said, "We don't have profit centers, we have experience centers. If the experience is right, the profit will follow." That's why I started this book by talking about community needs and using community organizing principles to meet those needs. No one's going to give you money because *you* need it. They will give you money only if you've done something valuable for *them*. Work on that, and the money will come.

How will it come? News publishers typically earn income from one or more of these three sources:

- Advertising
- Direct payments
- Grants and donations

Advertising

Newspapers and TV news programs historically have earned almost all of their income from advertising. TV broadcasts run commercials. Newspapers run display ads. But those haven't been the only ways that news publishers have made money through advertising. Decades ago, networks TV news broadcasts made money from product placement, by placing a certain brand of cigarette on their announcers' desks. Local newspapers profited from classified advertising, as readers looking to sell homes, cars, furniture or whatever placed text ads in the back of the local paper.

The federal government killed the cigarette ads, and Craigslist killed the paid classified ad business. Today, businesses can use social media such as Facebook and Twitter to connect directly with their customers more often than ever before, without having to buy ads to do it. But a business that's happy with reaching only its current customers — one that doesn't want to expand — is a business that probably won't be in business very long. That's why businesses continue to spend billions of dollars a year on advertising, trying to reach and attract new customers. So long as businesses need to reach new customers, they'll be willing to pay people with an audience for the opportunity to reach those readers and viewers.

Your audience determines what types of ads you'll be able to sell and to which advertisers you will be able to sell them. Later in the book, we'll talk about the importance of audience measurement — ways that you can determine who's reading your publication and how often. You'll need that data in order to make a convincing sales pitch to potential advertisers. Remember: ultimately, smart advertisers care more about whom you're reaching than what you're saying as a publisher.

You can get advertisers for your publication in two ways: By selling ads directly to advertisers or by participating in an ad network. Knowing the strengths and weaknesses of each approach will allow you to maximize the amount of money you make relative to the amount of time you spend working on advertising.

If the idea of selling ads makes you uncomfortable, participating in an ad network frees you from ever having to do that. Networks such as Google's AdSense <http://www.google.com/adsense> simply give you some computer code to place on your webpages (we'll talk later about code for webpages). The network handles all the sales and billing, leaving you only to collect the checks. The network keeps a cut of all the revenue it makes, sending you the rest.

Networks work best for publishers whose audiences are attractive to large national and international advertisers, selling in big-money industries. These large advertisers don't want to waste time dealing with the thousands of small publishers out there and prefer to place their online ads through a limited number of big networks that then place those ads on those thousands of smaller, niche-focused websites.

We use Google's AdSense network to deliver ads on ThemeParkInsider.com. An ad network is perfect for this site, which attracts a global audience of people planning family vacations that can costs thousands of dollars. Travel is a multi-billion dollar industry, and ThemeParkInsider.com readers collectively spend nearly $3 billion a year on theme park vacations, according to a random-sample survey of our readers. But even with all that money at stake, it's easier for us to reach advertisers such as Disney, Universal, Delta and American Express through Google than it would be to pitch, close and service those advertisers on our own.

Ad networks work best for niche-topic sites in lucrative niches (such as travel), that reach a national or global audience. Ad networks are terrible for sites whose audiences appeal primarily to smaller advertisers, "mom and pop" family-owned businesses that would get lost trying to compete in the global ad networks with big businesses such as Disney and American Express.

AdSense brought in less than one-tenth the revenue for Violinist.com as it did for ThemeParkInsider.com, despite the fact that both sites had about the same size audience. That's because businesses that need to reach violinists aren't huge public companies like Delta. They tend to be individually- or family-owned shops, selling to much smaller customer bases. We needed to sell to these advertisers directly and not rely on Google to sell our ads for us.

Once we made the decision to sell ads directly to advertisers, we realized that we needed to figure out how to price our ads. It turns out that there are several ways to do that.

The simplest way is to create an ad space on your page and charge an advertiser a fixed amount of money each month (or week or other period of time) to place its ad there. That works fine if you've only got a couple of advertisers, but what can you do when you've found a dozen businesses who want to advertise on your site? You can either clutter your page with a dozen advertisements, or you can rotate the ads into a limited number of spaces.

Almost all major websites now use the rotation system for placing ads on their sites. But even then, you've got multiple options on how to price ads. You can charge an advertisers based on the number of times you showed your readers the ad. (That's called a **CPM** system, for cost per thousand impressions — "M" being the Roman numeral for 1,000.) Or you can charge an advertiser based on the number of times people clicked on its ad. (That's called a **CPC** system, for cost per click.) Or you can charge advertisers a cut of their revenue they make from each reader you send them via the ads. (That's called either a **Commission** system or a **CPA** system, for cost per action.)

Don't worry about managing all these different sales options. Free software tools are available that will handle rotating ads on your site and keeping track of clicks. We'll talk more about that when we get into the technical details of how to publish a website.

Don't forget your customers either. Many small business owners will tune out when you start explaining complicated ad options. As online publisher Mark Potts said during one of our KDMC News Entrepreneur Boot Camps, "most local advertisers can't spell 'CPM'." So you've got to give them an option that they can understand and will embrace.

On Violinist.com, we started a business directory page, where we charged advertisers a few hundred dollars to have a listing for 12 months. Advertisers have a page they can go to and see their ad, without having to wait for it to show up in a banner ad rotation. It's easy to understand, and readers like having a page where they can go to find businesses selling various instruments, accessories and services, when they're in the market to buy right now.

With the directory, we've signed up more than dozen additional advertisers, some who couldn't afford large banner-ad campaigns on Violinist.com. We've also earned additional income from banner advertisers who realize that directory listings are great for reaching customers who want to buy immediately, while banners are better for creating brand awareness among readers who might not be in the market for a purchase now, but probably will be sometime in the future.

Other publishers are using the old "product placement" concept and selling "sponsored posts" in their blogs, where advertisers pay to run specific messages in a blog post. Whether you're running a sponsored post, a banner ad or a directory, do be sure that your site's design effectively tells readers what content on the page is paid advertising, and what's coming from you or from other readers. Deceiving an audience is a great way to lose it forever. Don't do that.

Be careful if someone offers to buy a link on your website. Google and other search engines have said they will penalize websites that buy or sell links in an effort to boost a site's position in their search engine results. It's okay to sell links, but you should note that they are paid links, and you should use some special coding in those links (a *rel="nofollow"* tag — again, we'll talk about that later) to keep you out of trouble with the search engines. If you follow those steps, many of those would-be advertisers trying to buy links won't bother with you, because they *are* trying to game the search engines. Consider yourself lucky to not get advertisers like that and let 'em go.

Ultimately, it's again all about finding and alleviating a community need. Advertising allows you to connect your audience with businesses that need to reach beyond their current customer base. A well-targeted selection of advertisers also provides readers with additional information about businesses serving their community. Different forms of advertising allow you to fulfill different needs for those businesses. The more you know about these options — and the more creative you can be in coming up with fresh ones — the more advertising revenue you can earn for your publication.

Direct payments

With direct payments, your audience and customers become one — your readers pay you directly for your work. Magazines sell subscriptions. Cable television networks get a cut of your monthly bill. Readers buy books. (We should note again, though, that newspaper subscriptions rarely covered more than the cost of printing and distributing the paper. Advertising paid for the actual reporting.)

Many newspapers have tried — and failed — to convince readers to pay for access to their websites. But that doesn't mean that readers won't pay for content online. In fact, there's a huge and rapidly-growing market for paid online content.

It's eBooks.

If you want to do investigative reporting and write long-form storytelling, you need to be writing and selling eBooks in addition to publishing a website. You don't need a publishing deal, either. Online booksellers such as Amazon, Barnes and Noble and Apple's iBookstore allow you to sell your eBooks through them as an independent publisher.

Amazon's commission structure for publishers pays you the maximum percentage (70 percent) for eBooks sold between $2.99 and $9.99. Let's say that you're making a very ambitious $20 CPM selling ads on your website. (That's $20 in revenue for every 1,000 page views on your site.) A reader would need to read more than 100 pages on your website for you to earn as much money from that reader as you would from the commission on the sale of a single $2.99 eBook. Given that most nonfiction eBooks sell for more than $2.99, and that most websites earn less than a $20 CPM from their ads, and that most readers read way fewer than 100 pages on a given website in a month, the profit margins for eBooks look even better.

Our first eBook, *Stories from a Theme Park Insider*, was simply a collection of blog posts and reader responses from ThemeParkInsider.com. We'd been running a weekly feature where I shared a story about my time working as an attraction host at Walt Disney World's Magic Kingdom, and many readers who's also worked in theme parks responded with stories of their own. I selected what I thought were the funniest or most touching stories and edited them into an eBook of about 35,000 words.

I initially priced the book at $3.99 and offered it for sale through several online retailers. Within a month, the eBook had reached number two on Apple's bestseller list in the travel category and reached the top 20 among all travel books (eBooks and print) on Amazon. Initial sales to my website readers helped the book get established on Amazon, so that it began recommending the book to readers of similar titles. That sold additional copies of the book, helping it move up the bestseller lists in several categories, attracting more attention and driving more sales.

Not only did I make money on those sales, the book also

helped introduce the website to those new readers, many of whom then became regular readers of the site. So eBooks not only provide an additional source of revenue for your publishing business, they're an additional source of publicity for your website, too.

Ebooks aren't the only way to make money from direct sales. Start-up news sites such as Paidcontent.org and NewWest have pioneered the use of offline events to earn revenue. As you build a community of readers on your site, it's possible — even likely — that many of these readers will want to get together and see each other in "real life." Readers might be willing to pay for the opportunity to attend an event with other readers and popular writers from your site. Event management is a much different skill than news publishing, but like publishing, it can fulfill an audience need.

Sometimes, you won't even need to do the planning yourself. If your community grows passionate enough about itself, some readers might even step up to do the organizing work for you. That's what happened on the political blog site DailyKos, where readers initiated and planned the first annual "YearlyKos" conference of website readers. Today, that event has grown into Netroots Nation, one of America's largest annual gatherings of progressive political activists.

Even if you don't plan a conference or event, your readers might be willing to pay to self-identify with your community. Print up some T-shirts or tote bags and you can make some extra bucks for your site while increasing its visibility within your target community. That's another form of direct payment revenue available to you.

Grants and donations

Grants and donations are direct payments made to you, but not in exchange for a specific product or service. That doesn't mean you won't be expected to provide something in return to the people giving you money, though. While unsolicited donations come with no strings attached, they rarely provide more than a sprinkling of cash for your ongoing operations.

Some publishers have found success using sites such as Kickstarter <http://www.kickstarter.com>, Indiegogo <http://www.indiegogo.com> and Spot.us <http://www.spot.us> to raise money from readers to fund specific projects. One of our KDMC News Entrepreneur Boot Camp alumnae, Laura Amico, raised more than $47,000 on Kickstarter to help train and pay student interns to help run the Homicide Watch project she launched with her husband <http://homicidewatch.org>. To raise donations for her project, Amico was able to draw upon a large and loyal following that Homicide Watch had attracted over the years. So while sites such as Kickstarter can help a publication with an established community of followers expand to another level of service, it might be tough for a start-up, with no following or name recognition, to raise significant amounts of money through these donation sites.

Grants can provide substantial operating income for a website, even a start-up, but going after and getting grants can demand huge amounts of time and effort. In almost all cases, in order to get grant funding for your publication, you will have to organize as a non-profit. I've written this book for individuals looking to start for-profit publishing businesses, so I won't go into all the work involved in setting up a non-profit, which includes appointing a board of directors and filing a whole bunch more tax forms than you would if you were to run a regular, for-profit business.

Many would-be publishers decide to go the non-profit route because they believe that means they won't have to worry about money. They're wrong. Again, non-profit is a tax status, not a business model. All the lessons in this book, about identifying and meeting needs, finding and retaining customers, building audience and community — they all apply to anyone running a non-profit publishing business, too. The only differences are that your customers would be the non-profit foundations that provide your grants and the tax forms you have to file throughout the year to report your income. Also, at the end of the year, if you end up with more money that you spent, you don't get to keep it for yourself. That's what "non-profit" means, after all. If you're running a for-profit business, you've got less paperwork to deal with and the money left over at the end of the year is all yours.

That's not to say you shouldn't make it easy for people to donate money to you if they feel like it. Or that you shouldn't develop business relationships with non-profits trying to reach your audience. It takes almost no work to set up a business account on PayPal and to slap a "Donate" button on your website. In fact, on Violinist.com, we use the PayPal "Donate" button to process credit card payments from our advertisers as well as to accept (non-tax-deductible) donations from readers. And while a non-profit foundation might not be able to give your for-profit website a grant, there's nothing stopping it from buying an ad on your site, should it want to reach your audience to promote something the foundation is doing.

Non-profits frequently organize conferences and events for which they pay knowledgeable speakers to participate. If foundations see you as a smart source on the community you cover, they might invite you, too. Speaking at events can be a great way to supplement your income as a publisher, or at the very least, to get some free travel to events around the nation or the world.

Investments and loans

Advertising, direct payments, grants and donations provide income to a website that's up and running. But what about before you launch? How can you get the money you need to live while you're doing the prep work to design and launch your website?

If you've got a strong track record in your community and can sweet-talk people, you might be able to sell some ads or land a grant before you launch. But most funders want to see that you can build an audience before they're willing to pay to access it. That leaves you with a couple other options.

Many tech start-ups seek investors before launching their sites. The pitch venture capitals and angel investors for money, often in exchange for a percentage of ownership in the company. To pursue this route, you'll likely need to incorporate, and you'll have to have a concept that can scale into a lucrative business, typically with income well into the hundreds of thousands of dollars a year — probably more than that. Local news websites don't fit that model, and won't get a moment of a venture capitalist's time. But a strong, well-focused niche website aimed at an affluent, global audience might attract investor funding.

For most would-be publishers, loans are probably your better bet. Talk to people in the small business department of your bank or credit union. They can talk you through the process of applying for a small business loan, or help you find you another type of loan if those aren't available to you. Bank or credit union employees also can help you set up a dedicated account for your new business — which is wonderfully helpful at tax time. They'll also help you set up a "fictitious business name" or "doing business as" declaration. Whatever that's called in your state, it's a legal requirement for people who are doing business under a name other than their own — as you will be when you launch a website. Even if you don't incorporate your publishing business, you'll need this business name declaration. (We'll review the steps you'll need to take to set up and launch your publishing business in Chapter 6.)

So let's talk about expenses

Okay, that was the fun side of learning about money — the income. Now, let's talk about the hard part — letting your money go. Obviously, the idea is to spend less money than you take in —

so much less that you have enough money left over to support yourself and your family. After all, for an independent start-up business, what you have left over after paying your expenses is your salary.

Ultimately, your customers decide how much money you'll take in. What they're willing to pay is what you'll make. So if you want to maximize your income, the easiest way is to control your expenses. Fortunately, that's easy to do in online publishing. Almost everything you need to publish you can get for free or for very little money: website hosting, a publishing system, a domain name, even your site's content.

As an independent publisher, you don't have access to a corporate expense account. Every dollar you spend on your business is coming out of your pocket. Start by working out of your home (which might entitle you to a tax deduction if you rent). Use a free blogging tool, such as Blogger or WordPress.com, to get a presence online and start building an audience. Use personal connections and social media to publicize your site.

Don't blow money on an office, a dedicated Web server, programmers or anything else a Fortune 500 company would buy to launch a website. Unless you've lined up several hundred thousand dollars in money from venture capitalists, smother your dreams of acting like a CEO and hiring a staff to run your new publication. If you want to make money, you're going to start by doing it all yourself.

Your family can help, especially if they'll work for free. In fact, your family should help with your new business. You won't be able to put the time, effort and attention into your business that it will demand if you don't have your family's full support. Involving them in the project, wherever they can help, is a great way to get that support.

My wife, a professional symphony violinist, edits Violinist.com. My son, who fell in love with filmmaking and video editing at a young age, shoots and edits video for our websites. That makes what could have been *my* business into *our* business — extending the size and scope of our publications and allowing us to reach more people and make more money than we would if I'd been doing everything myself.

Bringing family members into the business means that work time becomes family time, too, allowing you to spend extra time on the business without pulling you away from your loved ones. For the past several summers, my family has taken long vacations that always involve trips to theme parks, as well as visits to people in the violin world. By working for ourselves, we can hit the road for a month or more during the kids' summer vacation. We don't have to worry about getting vacation time from our boss. Publishing websites means that we can work wherever there's an Internet connection, which is just about anywhere these days. So we take our work on the road for weeks at a time during the summer, allowing us to spend more time with our children that we ever could working in a newspaper's newsroom.

Before you do anything, though, buy a paper notebook or create a file on your computer where you will keep track of everything you spend in creating and running your business. Every stamp, every box of computer paper, every pen, everything. Creating a separate bank account, with a separate credit/debit card, for your business also can help you keep accurate records tracking your spending. You can deduct most of your expenses from your business income when you file your income taxes, so failure to track expenses will cost you money on your tax bill. It also blinds you to how your business is running. You'll want to know what spending is helping you raise income, and what is not.

If you're worried about doing the math to keep track of those expenses, don't be. Spreadsheets can do many of the calculations for you. One of my first websites was a tutorial for math-phobic journalists called *Statistics Every Writer Should Know*. It offered plain-English explanations of some basic math terms, helpful in both news reporting and business management. I've included an updated version of that tutorial as an appendix in this book, to help you master some of the basic math skills you'll need as an online publisher.

As your business grows, you'll need to make smart decisions about where you spend your time and money to best grow the business for the future. If you don't have accurate information about your spending and income, you'll be making those decisions in the dark, increasing the chance you'll fail to make the decision that pays off best for you and your family. Keep accurate records.

EXERCISE

How much do you spend on content? For the next week, keep track of all your media spending. How much will you spend on books, magazines, newspapers, eBooks, music downloads, concerts, going to or renting movies? Keep track of all those.

Mark down every time you click an ad online, too, as well as what site you were on and what the ad was for. Then note every time you phone or visit a store after seeing an ad in print, on TV or radio, or on a billboard.

At the end of the week, write up a short report noting how much money you spent on media and how much you spent on each type: print books, newspapers, magazines, going to the movies, renting movies, buying eBooks, movies, music, etc. Then write another short report summarizing how you acted on ads you saw over the week, including online, print, broadcast and out-of-home ads.

Think about that spending and those clicks when you start selling ads and media. You should know how consumers react to the ad products you'll soon be trying to sell, and you can start by documenting your own reactions.

4 ANALYZE THE MARKET AND YOUR COMPETITION

In the first chapter, I asked you to think about the community you want to cover and the unmet needs in that community. Now that you know a little bit more about the way that online publications earn money, it's time to take another look at the needs you identified. Given what you know now about potential sources of income for your site, do you think the needs you've identified are big enough that people will pay you money if you successfully address them?

It's okay to express some doubt here. The world's filled with unresolved need. If you don't think you can make one idea work, move on to another one. Remember that the final step in community organizing is "repeat." So far in the book, I've told you a bit about my successful websites — ThemeParkInsider.com and Violinist.com. I've not mentioned the duds that didn't work:

- An online birth announcement site that I should have sold for whatever I could have gotten before Facebook and blogging sites allowed people better ways to share photos and personal news with family and friends.

- An advice site where people could submit and vote on short nuggets of advice on any topic. It might have worked had a bothered to learn how to write an API [application programming interface] so other Web publishers could include my site's data and voting tool on their websites and publishing services. Without that expanded distribution, the site never reached critical mass.

- A ThemeParkInsider.com-like rating-and-review site for Las Vegas, where I've never lived. Without a local editor providing daily insight and leadership, no one in that community stepped up to participate, leaving the site to stumble along with a few tourists like myself blathering about stuff we didn't know that well.

In every case, I failed to connect with a specific community and address a particular unresolved need. The birth announcement site came closest, but as a new parent with a full-time job at a newspaper, I didn't put the time into the site to expand it into a "new and expecting parent" portal that really could have connected and served that huge, ever-changing and, let's face it, quite financially active community. So the site limped along as a part-time venture until a technological disruption — social media — finally killed its meager traffic by better serving the one need I did meet (a place to post your newborn's picture).

The advice site lacked focus. It was a neat little tool but I never identified a specific pain for it to address. It was just tech for tech's sake — a lousy excuse for a business. And it wasn't very powerful or sophisticated tech. Had I developed an API, I could have offered it to other publishers as a resolution to *their* need for a nifty widget that aggregated, evaluated and prioritized readers' tips on whatever those sites covered. But I didn't make that connection, and the site just limped along for a while until I decided to save a few bucks and not renew the domain name.

The Vegas site failed because I wasn't part of that community, and I failed to build an action team that was. I simply didn't know enough about Las Vegas to make my site any more authoritative than any other tourists' blog posts about trips to the city.

ThemeParkInsider.com and Violinist.com worked because we were covering communities we knew well as members of those communities. We found and addressed real, unsolved needs in those communities and proved to other people in those communities that we had the expertise and authority to help.

What can you offer people in the community you wish to serve? In analyzing the community do not forget to analyze your potential role within that community as well. What expertise, experience and authority will you bring to the website? Why should anyone listen to what you say?

Remember your pitch: "Why are you the one who can do this?" That's a two-part question. You'll need to answer *why* you can do this, and why you are the *best* one to do it, as well. If many people in the community share your same skill set — and remember that some of them might be publishing websites, too — what will make your site so unique that someone would want to spend time or money on it?

If you are planning to cover a geographic community, get out a map and draw a line around the specific geographic area that you plan to cover. No matter what community you plan to cover — geographic, topical, or some combination of both — you should be as specific as possible in defining it for yourself. Without a strong definition of your community, you can't hope to analyze it.

When defining a geographic community to cover, I recommend you start with elementary school attendance zone boundaries. (Go to your local school district website to find them.) The average reader in any community spends more time in his or her life engaging with the local schools than with any other civic institution, whether it be as a student, a parent of a student, or both. Schools and communities define one another. Choose a mix of contiguous school attendance zones that provide you with a critical mass of both active consumers and local businesses willing to pay to reach them. But don't choose so many that you won't be able to cover them all effectively. Remember my Las Vegas mistake.

How well do you know your community? I've lived in Pasadena, California for more than 12 years. But every Sunday, when I go to church, it's to the same congregation. Yet hundreds more faith communities meet every week in my town. My children have attended the three largest public schools in the local district. Yet the district includes two dozen other schools, and several private schools attract kids from the community, too. I go to a farmer's market almost every Saturday morning, but three others set up each week around the city. I wrote several thousand words of this book in a local coffee shop, but hundreds of other people hang out in dozens of other coffee shops around town.

So no matter how well you think you're getting around town and talking with people, chances are that many, many, many other people are talking, sharing and working in other places around the community that you rarely, if ever, visit. Use your new project as an excuse to break your routine and discover new parts of your community. When was the last time you went to a school board or city council meeting? I'll bet there are several volunteer organizations in town that could use a hand. Ask your friends who are active in local organizations if you can tag along to their next meeting or event. People love to make connections. Make yourself available and see what new parts of your community you can discover. You might find opportunities you didn't know were there. At the very least, you can get a better sense of whether the need you had hoped to address is enough of a need to support your business.

During our News Entrepreneur Boot Camps, O'Malia showed our campers what he called a "Feasibility Funnel" for determining if an an idea could become a working, profitable business. You can find a complete explanation of the Feasibility Funnel in O'Malia's book, *The Entrepreneurial Journey* [Bradywine Publishing

Company, 2000]. (You can pick up a used copy on Amazon.)

O'Malia's not a journalist or a publisher, but he has years of experience launching new companies and studying successful start-ups. Even though his Feasibility Funnel wasn't designed specifically with online news businesses in mind, I find it a useful tool for analyzing a community in preparation for launching a news website business. These are questions you need to answer as you analyze the community, to prepare you to build the team and action plan you'll need to serve that community as we move through the community organizing process.

O'Malia's first step in the Feasibility Funnel is *Industry Knowledge.* Maybe you've worked at a newspaper and are looking to start out on your own. Maybe you are a journalism student, looking to get a head start in the business. Maybe you've never worked in publishing before, but you've read the news on a daily basis and see a need that other publications aren't filling.

No matter your background, the more you read, watch and interact online, they better feel you'll have for what works — and what doesn't — in an online publication. Approach your idea as a consumer. Would you want to read that site? Really? Are you trying to create the sort of site people will come to in the future, or are you simply trying to recreate something from the past, something the market is rejecting? The more you know about where the industry has been, where it is now, and where it is heading, the more likely you are to develop something that will gain readers as time goes on, instead of losing them.

O'Malia's second step is *Concept Recognition.* He defines a business concept as an idea that has a defined customer, a benefit to that customer and defined sales and distribution channels to deliver that benefit. In news publishing, the customer is the advertiser or funder who writes you the checks. The benefit is the exposure to interested readers — the audience — who will support the customer. And the channel is the publication that connects the audience with the customer.

Next up: **Market Risk**. Who is your competition? Who are *their* customers, and how are you going to do a better job of meeting customer needs than your competitors are doing?

What are the **Distribution Risks** of your idea? Can you get your content to your readers? Web publishing is well established at this point, but don't be naive and think that means you won't encounter distribution risks. Will the company you choose to host your website be able to keep it up and active 24/7? Will your publishing system be able to withstand hacker attacks? What about trolls and spammers who will try to exploit your community? The distribution risks of online publishing provide one of the big reasons why I'm looking to eBooks as a new revenue channel for our publishing business. With eBooks, you don't have to worry about spammers corrupting your discussion forums, hackers taking down your website or server crashes. If you can identify multiple potential distribution channels for your work (e.g. Web, eBooks, social media, etc.), you can minimize the overall risk to your business from a specific distribution risk in any one channel.

O'Malia's fifth step in his Feasibility Funnel is **Benefit Risk**. He writes: "a benefit is what your offering does *for* your customer — not what it *does*. Clearly customers need to know *what you do*, there is no argument about this. But it is more important that they know *what you do for them*." [p.154] Newspapers thought they were in the business of selling display and classified ads. They forgot that they really were in the business of delivering potential customers to advertisers. Will you be able to see benefit risks as they emerge, and adapt your business as needed?

The final step in the Feasibility Funnel is **Financial Risks**. Where will you get the money you need to launch your business? Will you run out after you launch? One great quality of online publishing (for you, at least, if not for established publishers looking to hang on to their market share) is that it costs next to nothing to launch. In Chapter 6 we'll go over a start-up checklist that will allow you to get a site up and running for as little as under

$100. The real financial risk in the online publishing industry is not cash — it's something else of great value: time. Will you have the time you need to spend researching, writing and interacting with readers? The time to identify, pitch, close and communicate with advertisers? The time to promote your website, edit eBooks, arrange events or whatever else you need to do to make your business financially viable? An action team can help save your bacon here, and we'll talk in greater detail about building that in the next chapter.

If your idea can survive each of those steps, you might have yourself a workable concept.

Now let's get to our exercise and see how your idea holds up. It's time to take a look at your competition. This is the "reality check" that will tell you if there's a market for what you hope to do, and if there's room in that market for you. Ready? This assignment's as easy as surfing the Internet and taking notes. Let's get started!

As you do the following exercise, if at any point you decide your idea isn't going to work — don't quit and give up your dream of starting a publishing business. Just go back to Chapter 1 and find another need. Just because one idea didn't pan out doesn't mean you can't earn a living through publishing. It just means that you need to find another need — one that can make it through the Feasibility Funnel.

EXERCISE

Find three websites you believe are serving the same audience you want to reach. They can be slick, big-business websites or simple, one-person blogs. Try to find the ones that are best connecting with the readers you hope to serve. When in doubt, go with the sites that most appeal to you, as a member of the community you want to serve.

For each website, collect the following information:

- The name of the website and its URL (website address)
- A short description of the specific niche community the site covers (the name of the neighborhood, or town, or the topic it covers)
- The site's average number of unique readers each month
- How the site makes money: ads, underwriters, etc.
- If the site displays ads, find the site's "rate card" — the prices the site charges for its ads.
- Make a list of all the site's current advertisers and/or funders.
- Estimate how much of the site's content comes from its staff, how much from readers, and how much is copied from elsewhere on the Internet.
- Find how many people work on the site — how many of them are paid, and how many are full-time employees?

Click around the website to find an "About Us" page, or a page for potential advertisers. Those pages usually include much of this information. You also can find site traffic information from Quantcast.com and Compete.com. Though that information is not always accurate, it's usually good enough to give you a rough idea of a website's size. You can create a list of a site's advertisers simply by clicking around and making a list of all the ads you see on the site. If you see a lot of ads for "big name" brands and companies that aren't directly related to the community the site covers, the website probably is using an ad network, in addition to or instead of selling its own ads. For your own list, focus just on the local or community advertisers.

If all else fails, just call or email the people running the site and ask about their ad rates. Tell them that you're thinking about starting a business in the community and you're trying to get an idea about what your publicity costs might be. You don't have to tell them what your business will be. And you wouldn't be lying, either. You *are* thinking about starting a local business, and you *are* trying to get an idea of what the costs to advertise in the community will be. (Heck, if it makes you feel better, you might even think about buying an ad on their site to promote your's when you launch. There's nothing stopping you, assuming they'd sell you the ad.)

5 BUILDING YOUR ACTION TEAM

As I have written before, no one goes into business alone. No one. You won't launch your business on your own, either. Even if you're planning to work as a staff of one, reporting and writing a website you designed yourself, you still won't be building your publication business alone.

First, your business won't last long without income. And that means you'll need customers. They will help build your business, too.

And no one's going to pay to support your publication or advertise on it if no one else is reading it. So you'll need an audience. They will help build your business, too.

Who will spread the word about your site? You won't build much of an audience if it's to be limited to your own personal contacts. Who will "Like" your publication on Facebook, and retweet your domain name on Twitter? Who will tell their friends, co-workers and family members about your site and encourage them to visit? Your advocates will. They will help build your business, too.

How will you design your website? What tools will you use — which design programs and coding languages? You couldn't design anything without the work of the teams that created them. They will build your business, too.

How will people access your website? Who's going to keep your Web server running 24/7? Who will maintain the routers that direct requests to your site and the backbones and Internet connections that deliver those requests and your site content in return? You'll need their support to build your business, too.

So even if you're planning to work as a solo, bootstrapping entrepreneur, taking no loans or investments from anyone and hiring no staff to help — you will need an action team to help you build this business.

Building an action team isn't a casting call. Don't just go looking for people to fill a certain number of specific roles in building your business. That's why building an action team comes *before* the action plan in our community organizing system. In building your action team, you should make yourself open to working with anyone who you believe can help you to meet your goal of addressing the needs in your community. Team comes first. Assign roles later.

We just stumbled into building our action team on ThemeParkInsider.com. When I started the website, I listed attractions only at the Disney and Universal theme parks I knew from living in Orlando and Los Angeles. But within a few months, readers were asking me to include other theme parks on the site, too. Some even volunteered to do the data-entry work for me, just so they could have the lists of rides and shows on the site to rate and review. Boom! They're on the action team. Some time later, a reader with graphic design experience volunteered to create a new logo for the website. Welcome to the action team! Over the years, readers have become tipsters, emailing me news and rumors they've heard about what will be happening in the parks they visit or where they work. They're on my action team, too.

Having that action team available has given me a deep bench of contributors that I can call upon to assume more formal roles, when I need them. Theme parks around the world send me invitations to new ride and show openings. While I try to get to the biggest ones at the most popular parks (always paying my own way to get there — even if the parks offer to cover my travel expenses), I don't have the time or the money to go to all of them. With my action team, I can call on readers who live near those parks, who've also demonstrated their ability to report and write on the site, to cover those events for us.

Publishers get in trouble when they get so hung up on the specifics of *what* they do — writing articles, selling banner ads, writing reports — that they forget *why* they're doing these things in the first place. Publishers get in trouble when they forget about the benefit they're supposed to be providing with all this work. By keeping an open mind and remaining flexible to suggestions, I built an action team of readers who were willing to volunteer to help the site. Some I put into formal roles right away. Others I kept in touch with and called up later. If I'd put my plan first and only looked for people who could have helped with my plan, I would have missed the chance to make connections that would help me take advantage of other opportunities in the future.

Open your eyes and ears and get out in the community. In the previous chapter, I asked you to go to meetings, get active in community groups and meet some new people in order to get a better sense of the community you want to serve. Don't think of that as a single exercise — something to do one time, because an author asked you to. Obviously, you won't have the time or the desire to keep up with every new group or cause you encounter, but if you're going to be an active, engaged community servant (and that's what you are, as a publisher), you will have to remain active and engaged in the community. Keep in the habit of engaging with new groups and causes from time to time. This will feed you with the tips that will keep your reports fresh, and it will keep you in contact with many potential new friends of your publication who can help on your action team, whether that's in formal or casual roles. Staying engaged will help you discover new opportunities for your business as well.

Don't be afraid to share what you're trying to do with the people you meet. Many would-be entrepreneurs are afraid to talk about their plans because they fear someone will steal their idea. Allow me to let you in on another secret about business:

Ideas are worthless. It's the execution of ideas that has value.

Consider a crucial scene from the Academy Award-winning movie *The Social Network*. The Winkelvoss twins have accused Mark Zuckerberg of stealing the idea for Facebook, which they say was theirs.

"If you had invented Facebook," the Zuckerberg character replies, "you would have invented Facebook."

Plenty of other people had come up with ideas for social networks. Heck, MySpace and Friendster had attracted millions of users before Facebook hit the scene in the mid-2000s. The Zuckerberg character's point was that the unique entity that is Facebook wasn't defined by the idea of creating another social network. It was defined by the unique code, design and functionality that Zuckerberg created. The *idea* of Facebook had no value — it was Zuckerberg's *execution* of Facebook that drew millions of users and made the website worth billions of dollars.

So don't worry that someone will steal your idea. If someone wants to take your idea and do a better job of executing it, they can do that just as easily a couple months after your launch. You'll be out of business either way. But if you can execute your idea better than a competitor, it doesn't matter if that person beats you to launch. You'll still win away their audience and customers.

(Which brings me to another important lesson about business: Don't sweat the competition. Focus on executing solutions to a community's need, and you'll do well enough.)

How will you execute these ideas? Again, you'll need that action team to help you. The more skills, experience, intelligence and connections you can call upon to help design, publish, promote and grow your publication, the more likely it will attract a large clientele of paying customers. Maybe you're a smart person who has a lot of these qualities yourself. But if you seek and find help, you'll have access to even more skills, experience, intelligence and connections in designing and implementing your plans.

One important member of your action team should be a mentor — an experienced entrepreneur with whom you can talk and share experiences, and from whom you can get some feedback. This person doesn't have to be in the online publishing industry, but you'll get more from a relationship with a mentor if you can share knowledge of the same industry.

Start your search for a mentor by thinking of the publications you admire most. What do you read on a daily basis? What do you wish your publication could be like? It doesn't have to be a publication covering your community. In fact, it's better if it isn't, given the competitiveness that would likely exist between you and a publisher covering the same thing. Think of a publication you like, then learn more about the people running it. Who are they, where are they from, and what do they do for the publication? Did they help start it, or did they join the publication later? You're looking for someone who helped start a publication that you admire, someone who already has taken the journey you are beginning, someone who would be willing to share his or her experiences along the way.

Two other great places to find potential mentors are the Online News Association <http://journalists.org> and the Block by Block Community News Network <http://www.blockbyblock.us>. These organizations include hundreds of online news publishers, many who founded the sites they're now running. The ONA includes website staff at many major newspapers and large independent news sites, while Block by

Block focuses more on smaller, community websites, often published by a single staff member. Some people belong to both organizations. (I've been a member of ONA and have worked with many Block by Block founders as part of the KDMC News Entrepreneur Boot Camps.)

When you find someone you think might be a good mentor for you, reach out with an email or phone call. Introduce yourself as someone who is starting an online publication and ask if you could talk sometime, for a few minutes, about starting a publication. *Do **not** use the word "mentor."* You wouldn't bring up marriage on a first date, so don't ask for anything more than a short conversation about starting a business. If you can meet in person, over coffee or lunch (you're buying), that's best. Think seriously about getting in the car or on a plane to meet the right potential mentor for you. After all, this is your future business, and having the right mentor is important. But a phone conversation is better than no conversation at all.

The purpose of this first talk is not to tell your potential mentor about yourself or what you're trying to do. It's to learn about the mentor. Ask about his or her journey — what led him or her into this business? What need did he or she see? How did he or she choose to address it? What changed along the way and how did he or she adapt? What has your mentor learned from the journey that your mentor wishes he or she had known at the beginning? What opportunities are he or she seeing now? How did he or she see these as opportunities? (Note that I did not ask "why" he or she sees these as opportunities. That's another question, and not nearly as interesting to you as learning *how* someone recognizes opportunity in her or his community.)

Chances are, if your potential mentor has worked in journalism before, he or she will try to interview *you*, and ask about your background and goals. Respond politely, but don't allow him or her to become the interviewer. End each response with a question of your own, so that you can get the answers about this person's journey that you need.

After your talk, follow up with a thank-you note or email. If the talk went well and your potential mentor seems open to more contact, keep in touch. Let him or her know about major milestones as you develop the business and ask questions when you've got something big where your mentor can help. Let the relationship develop.

It's okay to "date around," too. There's no legal requirement for mentorship monogamy. Reach out to as many people as you'd like, but don't be a spammer. Don't reach out to so many people that you can't follow through with them all. And never fail to thank people for their time.

Working in online media, your action team will need to include other businesses and organizations, as well as individuals. Consider the provider you select to host your website, the development community behind the tools you use to build the site and any advertising networks you employ on the site to be part of your action team, too. You won't be able to function without them. We'll learn more in the next chapter about the technical requirements of setting up a website, and I'll give you a checklist of tasks that you can follow as you assemble the technical members of your action team and implement their work as part of your action plan.

> **EXERCISE**
>
> Find and interview a potential mentor. Using the criteria above, find an individual who has successfully started an online publication, who you believe can help guide you along your way toward doing the same. Use the questions above to spark a conversation, then write up a report about your talk. This isn't intended for publication on your future website — or anywhere else. It's simply to record your conversation and help guide you in the future with one potential roadmap for starting a business. But it is a map you'll need to help guide you, so don't skimp on detail and pay close attention to the insight you find from your conversation.

6 ACTION PLAN: YOUR STARTUP CHECKLIST

I think my son started his first blog when he was eight.

Clearly, starting an online publication today doesn't require advanced education or technical training. Go to a site such as *http://www.blogger.com*, fill in a few blanks, and you've got a website. That's a fine way to start. You don't need to spend a lot of time and money building your own online publishing system if all you want is a simple blog. But if you're going to build a profitable, long-lasting business around your new website, you're going to need to offer something a bit more useful and engaging than what an eight-year-old can do.

So let's learn more about how websites work and the options you have in building one. A basic understanding of online architecture will help you when you are working with your action team and potential customers. It's okay to recognize that some people might know more than you about the technical side of the Internet but if you're going to work in this industry, you don't want to look like an idiot.

A website is simply a collection of documents and programs

that reside on a computer somewhere. On a very simple website, the site's webpages are individual documents on that computer, written in what's called Hypertext Markup Language, or **HTML**. Each of those webpage documents is identified by a unique name, called a Uniform Resource Locator, or **URL**. That computer will use what is called the Hypertext Transfer Protocol, or **HTTP**, to deliver a copy of that document to your computer when you ask for it. That's what allows you to read that webpage.

Here's an example of a URL:

http://www.robertniles.com/stats/stdev.shtml

When you type that into a Web browser (such as Safari or Chrome), you are asking your computer to use hypertext transfer protocol (the **http://** part) to make a request to the computer that hosts the **www.robertniles.com** website, to find the **stats** folder on that computer, and to deliver a copy of the **stdev.shtml** file inside the stats folder to your computer. The HTML code in that file contains the instructions to your browser that tell it what text and images to display for that webpage.

How does your HTTP request get to that computer? Your computer needs to be connected to the Internet, through some Internet Service Provider (**ISP**). Connections can be wireless, over a Wireless Fidelity (**WiFi**) network or a cellular data network, such a EDGE, 3G, 4G or LTE. Or they can be wired, such as a connection you might have at home or the office, perhaps using a cable, DSL or fiber optic network. Your request goes from your computer (or smartphone) to the ISP, which then routes it across what's called an Internet backbone connection to the ISP that hosts the computer you're trying to contact.

The computer you're trying to contact is running a piece of software called a Web server, which manages incoming connections and finds and returns those HTML files that other computers are requesting. The Web server knows where to send the page you requested because your computer (or smartphone) — like every other device connected to the Internet — has what's called an Internet Protocol number, or **IP address**.

An IP address looks like this — 10.11.14.10 — and it's assigned by your ISP. Depending upon your connection, your device might get a different IP each time you log online. The computer hosting the website you're trying to get has an IP address, too. In fact, the domain name of every website is simply an English-language alias for the domain's IP address. After all, it's much easier to remember www.violinist.com than it is to remember 67.199.102.3. (But if you really want to be a geek, you also can type a website's IP address into a browser, instead of its domain name. Go ahead and type http://67.199.102.3 into Safari or Internet Explorer and see what happens!)

An ISP uses what's called the Domain Name System (or **DNS**) to look up what IP address corresponds to a specific domain name, whenever you make a request. ISPs have Domain Name Servers that keep a record of all those domain names and IP addresses, so that they can find and make those connections as quickly as possible, usually within microseconds.

When you "buy" a domain name, you are actually just contracting with a domain name registrar to associate a particular domain name exclusively with a computer of your choosing (your website host) for a specific period of time, from one to 99 years.

In the Web's early days, whenever you wanted to make a change to your website, you would use File Transfer Protocol (**FTP**) to upload a new HTML document from your computer to the Web server hosting your website. You would use a piece of software called an FTP client to make that connection and transfer the files. Your website (ideally) would be protected by a username/password combination that would only allow you to make FTP connections to your Web server, even as it allowed everyone to use an HTTP connection to view the content of those files.

These days, websites typically are quite a bit more complex

than a simple collection of HTML documents sorted into folders on a Web server. Most major websites use a Content Management System (or **CMS**) that can create virtual HTML documents on the fly. Modern websites aren't simply a collection of unchanging (or "flat") documents anymore — they're computer programs that generate highly customizable webpages and online presentations, under the direction of their publishers of course.

The CMS should have a user-friendly interface that allows a publisher with no programming experience to create a highly sophisticated-looking website, with powerful functionality. Few publishers use every feature that a CMS can deliver. Part of your job as a publisher will be to pick which functions and tools you think will best allow you to address your readers' real needs. Only rarely will you use FTP to update a website these days. Almost always, you'll use the interface of your CMS to add or edit content on your website. (That's what's happening when you use a service such as Blogger. The Web forms you fill out to post an entry on Blogger are simply the user interface to Blogger's CMS.)

On modern websites, a URL can do more than just request a specific document on the server — it can pass information to the CMS that allows it to create a customized page on the fly. That way, a website publisher doesn't have to create a new HTML file for every new post he or she writes. Just use the CMS interface to input your story, which will be stored in a database on the server. The website CMS then can take a single story-template file on the server and plug in the content from any of those stories you've posted to create what looks to the reader like a regular webpage. Consider a URL such as this:

http://www.robertniles.com/story.php?article=1003&ad=4

That URL tells the Web server that hosts www.robertniles.com that it wants to display the article with the identification number 1003, using the story.php template. And, oh yeah, go ahead and show the ad from advertiser number 4 when creating this webpage, too.

A CMS can create pages customized to an individual reader, too. Websites can leave a short line of text — called a "**cookie**" — in the memory of a browser when a user visits a page on the site. Cookies usually store an identification number, which the website can use to customize content on the site for that individual reader.

Let's say a website records an identification number for each reader who visits the site. It does this by first asking the reader's Web browser if it is storing any cookies from that site. If the browser doesn't report a cookie, the website knows that the reader is a first-time visitor, and asks the browser to set a cookie from the site.

But if the browser already has a cookie from the site, it can report back to the website the identification number stored in the cookie. That way, the website knows that reader "100001" is back again and looking at the site.

A website can store in its own database a whole bunch of information about user number 100001, or any other visitor to the site. It could store the time that visitor last came to the site, allowing the website to show that visitor only new posts or comments since his or her last visit. If user number 100001 creates an account on the website, it could record if and when the user logs into the site, allowing the site to customize its display according to that user's preferences. The website also could track what user 100001 clicks on, and which pages he or she views, allowing the website to make a more educated guess about which types of ads the user might be most willing to click.

All major browsers allow users to control the setting of cookies, or to delete them altogether. But if a reader chooses not to allow cookies, he or she won't ever be able to log into a website, and every site online will treat that user like a first-time visitor.

> **TECH STUFF**
>
> If you're curious, here's what one example cookie looks like:
>
> .violinist.com TRUE /bakery FALSE 1999999999 VISITORID 100001
>
> What does that mean? Here's the technical explanation: This cookie says that it has been set by "violinist.com", which is the only Web domain that can read and act upon the cookie. The "TRUE" means that the cookie can be read via HTTP only, and the "/bakery" means that the cookie can be read by any webpage in the "bakery" directory on Violinist.com. The "FALSE" means that the reader doesn't need to be using a secure Internet connection for the website to read and act upon the cookie. The "1999999999" tells the browser when to delete this cookie. (It's the number of seconds since Jan. 1, 1970 at midnight GMT.) The "VISITORID" is the name of the variable that this cookie is storing, and "100001" is the value of the "VISITORID" variable.

A modern CMS will handle cookie management for you — it's not something that you'll need to set manually as a website publisher. But you should know what's happening "under the hood" of your CMS, to best be able to use its abilities to meet your community's needs as a publisher. As we move forward in this book — and as you move forward in your publishing business — I hope that you'll use this chapter to help you keep straight the alphabet soup of acronyms you'll find in online publishing: HTTP, URL, HTML, IP, ISP, DNS, FTP, CMS, etc. You'll see them again and again as you work in this field.

Now that you know how Internet publishing works, let's take a look at a checklist that will guide you through setting up an online publishing business. In October 2010, I wrote a post for OJR.org called "Thinking about starting an online news business? Here's your start-up checklist" <http://www.ojr.org/ojr/people/robert/201010/1893>, which I've updated for the list in this chapter. You don't need to complete all of these steps in the order they're presented, but you will need to finish some of them before you can move on to others. (For example, you have to pick a name before you can trademark it.) As always, read through the whole list before doing anything.

Let's get started!

The name

☐ Choose a name for your publication

People write entire books on this task alone, but hey, we've got other stuff to do here, so I'm going to cover this in two paragraphs. You'll want a name that people can remember, and that people easily will associate with the content of your site. If you're covering a specific geographic community, it makes sense to include the name of that community in the name of the publication. (It's not a requirement, of course. Perhaps there might be some other creative name that residents would associate with the community. Ultimately, it's up to your judgment.)

Short, easy-to-spell names are best. Your name should be as easy to say as it is to type in a browser's address bar. "Violinist.com" was the perfect name for a website covering violinists, but I registered that name way back in 1996. Perfect names are all gone now. So you'll need to get a little creative to find a good, easy-to-remember .com domain name that no one else has registered yet. Whatever you do, don't use a hyphen or other special character in your domain name. And I'd highly recommend you use a .com name, rather than some other domain extension, such as .net, as so many readers just assume that website names are followed by a ".com."

☐ Register your domain name

Once you've selected a name, don't hesitate to register it with a domain registrar, such as Hover.com, NameCheap.com or Gandi.net. Don't bother adding any of the hosting or e-mail options these companies might try to sell you as you register your domain. You'll figure out that later. If you can't decide between a handful of domain names, go ahead and register them all, then settle on one later. For a few bucks a year, it's worth securing several name options. Plus, registering extra names might keep those good alternative publication titles out of the hands of your future competitors. (How I wish I'd done that with all the theme park website domain names I considered!)

- [ ] Register a Twitter account

The inherent challenge with online publishing is reminding people to come to your webpage to read what's new. A website doesn't work like a daily newspaper, which you can deliver to readers' front doors. A few years ago, publishers used RSS feeds to deliver stories to readers, but Twitter and Facebook have replaced RSS as the go-to ways that millions of readers discover fresh news online. You might have a personal Twitter account, but you should also register one for your publication using the name you selected for the Web domain. Keep in mind that Twitter has a 15-character limit for account names. (That's why ThemeParkInsider.com is @themepark on Twitter.) And for future reference: Always remember which account you're logged into when you Tweet! It's just embarrassing to send violin Tweets to roller coaster fans, and vice versa. And it's potentially damaging to your business to send personal Tweets to your publication's followers. We'll talk more about conducting yourself as a public person in Chapter 8.

- [ ] Open a business checking account

No, you don't have any income yet, but you'll want a bank account as soon as you have a business name. Separating your business account from your personal accounts from day one will help you with accounting and income taxes. It'll also help you project a professional image to your customers, as having a business account will allow you to write and accept checks in the name of your publication, instead of having to do that in your own name. Doing business in your own name makes you look like you're running your site as a hobby, not as a business.

☐ Register a fictitious business name

The terminology varies from state to state: "Fictitious business name" or "Doing business as" [DBA]. This just means that you've set up a formal, registered business name, in lieu of incorporating. Banks or credit unions can help you set this up when you open your business checking account.

☐ Trademark your name

You can use a trademark lawyer to register your publication's name as a trademark, but that can be expensive. If you have some patience and can follow instructions well, you can register a trademark yourself, using the directions on the U.S. Patent and Trademark Office website <*http://www.uspto.gov/trademarks/basics/index.jsp*>. (I did it myself.) All of the paperwork can be filed online. Once you've applied, the process takes months, but the earlier you start, the earlier you will have your trademark in hand.

Getting operational

☐ Get a tax preparer

Unless you will be publishing a niche-topic website on tax preparation, you do not want to be wasting time researching all the tax implications of everything you'll be doing in business. Talk to an expert about this, instead. If you've done your own taxes in the past, your financial life is about to become much more complicated. You will need the help and advice of an expert to steer you through choosing the appropriate filing status, claiming the correct deductions and making the right quarterly tax payments on time. Look for a tax specialist in your community, since you might face local business taxes as a self-employed person that you never had to consider as an employee. Getting a tax preparer now will save you from suffering big financial — and possibly legal —

problems down the road. Eventually, if your business grows large enough, you might want to hire an accountant to handle all your income and expenses. But for now, start with a tax preparer.

☐ Find a place to do your work

When you work for yourself, you can work from anywhere. But you still need to work from *somewhere*. You can work out of your home (I still do), but you should set aside space that's just for your work. Having a set work space has a tax advantage if you rent, as you might be able to deduct part of your monthly rent payment as a business expense for that home office. Home office deductions are more complicated for home owners — your ability to claim a deduction might depend on whether your home is appreciating or declining in value. Also, in some communities, zoning rules might restrict what kind of work you can do legally in your home. Talk to your tax preparer about these issues. (See why I told you to get one?)

While a home office can be a great choice for a new business, since it won't cost you much extra money up front, as your business grows, you'll want to consider out-of-home office space. Not only does that allow you to reclaim your home for personal and family life, having a "real" office allows you a place to meet clients and hire help. A dedicated office also helps to show other businesses in the area that you're a serious participant in the local community, just like them. That can be a huge advantage for a "hyperlocal" website competing for local ad money.

☐ Buy insurance

You'll need extra insurance for your workspace and equipment. Check with your home owner's or renter's insurance company to see if you can add that onto your existing policy, or if you'll need to buy a new one. Pick a search engine and look up "libel insurance" to find a provider for that, too. You'll want protection if someone sues over something you wrote. Finally, visit the Online Media Network <*http://www.omln.org/*> before you go too far with your new business. They can be a great resource for you to help you avoid — or at least get through — legal entanglements in the course of your work.

Tech time

☐ Get equipment and software

As an online publisher, you'll need to be connected to the Internet, at all times, no matter where you go. So you'll need a smartphone or tablet with wireless Internet access that will allow you to update or edit your website whenever news breaks or flame wars erupt on your site. I use the latest iPhone because it provides me the instant online access I need, along with a mobile phone, a decent video and still photo camera and an audio recorder. (If the voice recorder allowed me to record phone calls, it'd be perfect.)

You won't want to write all your site updates on a cell phone, so pick a laptop computer, too. On it, you'll want, at minimum:

- A video editing program, such as iMovie, Final Cut or Adobe Premiere
- A photo editing program, such as Photoshop, GIMP or Pixelmator
- A calendar or task-management app. You do *not* want to be relying on memory, or little random slips of paper, to keep track of key dates and tasks as you move forward.
- A word processing program — ideally one that can work in HTML or Word, and has the ability to export to PDF (for eBooks). I use NeoOffice, for Mac.
- A spreadsheet, to keep track of your income and expenses. (Again, NeoOffice for me.)
- An FTP program, such as FileZilla or Fetch, for those rare instances when you need direct access to files on your Web

server.

- A variety of Web browsers — Safari, Firefox, Opera, Chrome and Internet Explorer — to test the display of your website.

Don't get a desktop computer — hold out for the laptop. When you travel to cover something for your website — and you inevitably will — you will want to have your "home" computer with you to do your work on the road. Don't mess with juggling a laptop and a desktop, paying for both and trying to keep the information on each in synch. Just stick with the laptop for everything.

I also like to keep several USB drives around to back up especially important files. (I don't buy them — I just reuse the ones I get as handout digital press releases at press events. But, hey, I'm cheap.) You might want to consider an external hard drive, such as Apple's Time Machine, for backups and additional storage, as well.

While digital cameras on cell phones keep getting better, for the best video and photo quality, you'll want to buy a digital SLR [single-lens reflex] camera. Get a compatible microphone for better audio quality on video, too. And a tripod is a must for focus and image stability.

Recently, I added an eyeglasses camera to my arsenal, as well. I chose a model from Pivothead <http://pivothead.com/>, which embeds an 8-megapixel 1080p video camera inside a pair of photochromic sunglasses. They're great for hands-free interviews and POV [point of view] shots. (I use them for roller coaster videos on ThemeParkInsider.com.) Just remember to keep your head very, very still — but if you can do that, your body makes an excellent tripod for image stability.

Finally, shop around and find a good quality, comfortable backpack that will hold your gear. I've been happy with the computer carriers from Outdoor Products <http://www.outdoorproducts.com>, but anything that works for you is a great pack.

☐ Pick a Content Management System

Okay, it's time for the biggie. Start by scrolling down to the bottom of the home page on the blogs and other websites you most like visiting and look for a little "Powered by [so-and-such]" line down there. The "[so-and-such]" will be the name of the site's CMS. If you get in the habit of looking for that information, you'll learn about your CMS options and get a feel for what they can do.

For a start-up news publication, stick with an established CMS — don't try to develop your own. Unless you are a programmer with some unique tricks you think will create value for your site's customers, you don't want to waste time and money creating a system to put text, video and photos online when so many people have done that already for you. Here are the names of and links to five popular, ready-to-go CMS options for publishing blogs and news websites:

- Blogger <*http://www.blogger.com*>
- WordPress <*http://wordpress.org*>
- Drupal <*http://drupal.org*>
- Joomla <*http://www.joomla.org*>
- Expression Engine <*http://expressionengine.com*>

Looking for some analysis of these options? Visit <*http://blog.pixelcrayons.com/cms/top-8-most-usable-cms-platforms*> for a write-up comparing WordPress, Drupal, Joomla and Expression Engine, along with a few other CMS options. Ultimately, you're looking for a system that helps you feel comfortable publishing. You want something that's easy for you to understand, so that you can focus on reporting, writing and interacting with readers instead of doing techie stuff to make the publishing system work. You'll also want a system that supports an easy-to-use ad management system, which is mandatory if you'll be an ad-supported website. You can find plenty of other blog publishing solutions online, but if they don't allow you to run your own ads, they're not appropriate for an ad-supported publishing business.

Make this decision in conjunction with the next decision on the checklist — selecting a hosting provider. If you will be using Blogger, that decision's made for you, as Blogger is also a hosting service. But for the other CMS options, you'll need a hosting provider that support the CMS software you choose. Keep reading for tips on doing that.

Do not make this decision alone. Reach out to your action team for advice. Perhaps your mentor has some experience with this decision and can help you. Many members of Block by Block and the Online News Association have faced the same decision and can share what they've learned working first-hand with these systems. LinkedIn has dozens of interest groups for online media professionals, with links to many articles analyzing the strengths and weaknesses of various content management systems. Do some reporting. Ultimately, your decision on a CMS will not make or break your business. Your ability to connect with and meet the needs of customers will determine how well you succeed. But using a CMS that works for you can help you escape some of the technical hassles that will distract you from the core work of serving your community.

☐ Select a hosting provider

You'll want a hosting provider with extensive experience supporting the CMS you've selected, which is why I listed that step first. Again, rely on recommendations from colleagues and friends to guide you. A great place to learn about hosting providers is the user support forums for each CMS, which you will find linked from their websites, which I listed above. Many CMS development teams maintain a list of preferred hosting providers, which they include on the CMS's website. Note that if you choose Blogger, you can skip this step, as you're stuck with the blogspot.com host if you use that content management system.

☐ Install publishing system, if necessary

Depending upon the hosting package you select, you might need to install the CMS software yourself. Delve into your hosting provider's support forums or throw yourself upon the mercy of its support staff. If your hosting provider doesn't have either online support forums or a helpful support staff, you've picked the wrong host.

Starting up

Here are 10 remaining steps you'll need to complete during your journey to launch. Some of these steps are quick, one-time tasks you can handle yourself. Others might require finding outside help. And others are steps you'll revisit and re-do again and again as you maintain your site over the years. Again, don't forget to reach out to your action team for advice, if you ever get stuck along the way.

☐ Design Web templates

Once you have a CMS, you'll need to customize it to reflect your publication. Select an available theme or design your own by modifying the HTML template files that came with the CMS. If you have no clue how to do that, you'll be best off sticking with a pre-designed template or hiring a designer to do this work for you. If you're interested in learning more about the HTML that drives your website, you can find a useful introduction to HTML and website interface design at <*http://learn.shayhowe.com/html-css/*>.

Plan to revisit your website design frequently in your first year, and then every couple years after that. You can find dozens of books focused solely on website design, but I think the best way to learn is to pay attention to the websites you most like and note how they do things — the alignment of features on the page, their use of color and typography, etc. It's considered bad form to lift someone else's HTML code directly, but everyone in this industry finds inspiration and guidance from looking at what others are doing online.

When selecting or designing site templates, remember mobile devices. More than 20 percent of our readers on ThemeParkInsider.com and Violinist.com visit using mobile devices, such as iPhones and iPads. These two leading mobile devices do not support Flash animation, so we don't use Flash on our websites, and we discourage our advertisers from using Flash ads. (If they do want a Flash ad, we ask that they provide an alternate image in .JPG format that we can display in that space for our mobile readers.)

Several years ago, Web publishers needed to create stripped-down alternate versions of their websites to display on tiny, underpowered mobile phones. Today, the vast majority of your mobile visitors will be coming to your site via smartphones and tablets that can display full website designs. Screen size remains an issue, though, especially on iPhones. But on our websites, we've chosen to use basic, simple HTML designs that degrade gracefully on smaller smartphone screens, instead of creating an alternate mobile design. This allows our ads to display to mobile readers as well, who happen to click on those ads at a higher rate than readers using "traditional" devices. If you do want to use a mobile-only design, most CMSs support them, and implementing one can be as easy as selecting a few options on your setup. Look for a mobile design option that includes ads, unless you're willing to throw away a large chunk of revenue-producing traffic.

Don't worry about building apps for your publication, especially before launch. Remember this simple rule: Apps are for functionality — webpages and eBooks are for content. If customers have a specific need that you'll fulfill through programming, consider an app to do that. If you're fulfilling a need through storytelling, you want to produce an eBook (for long stories) or a website (for shorter ones), instead. Reserve app development for later projects that require readers to search or otherwise take an active role in managing data, as opposed to simply reading your narrative content.

☐ Select a Web traffic analytic system and install tracking code in Web template

We'll learn in Chapter 9 about the importance of tracking your website's traffic. I use Google Analytics <http://analytics.google.com>. It's free and provides more than enough data for a start-up's needs.

☐ Select an ad management system and install the code

Again, in Chapter 9 we'll learn about the ways that publishers can show advertisers how much readers are engaging with their ads. You'll need an ad management system to do this for you, but free and powerful systems are readily available. I use Google's Doubleclick for Publishers system <http://www.google.com/dfp>, which not only allows me to sell my own ads, but also allows me to display Google's AdSense ads in ad spots I don't sell.

☐ Create a Facebook page for your publication

Go to <http://www.facebook.com/pages> and click the "Create a Page" button. You'll need to get 25 fans for your page before you can select a shortcut URL for the page (e.g. <http://www.facebook.com/themeparkinsider>). Be sure to add a prominent link to your Facebook page within your site template and update it with the shortcut link once you've selected it.

Once you've created a Facebook page, you might consider using some of Facebook's developer tools to enhance the functionality of your website and to promote your Facebook page. Visit <http://developers.facebook.com> for more information.

☐ Create an e-mail list and online subscription form

In addition to alerting readers about new content via Facebook and Twitter, don't forget about good ol' email newsletters. I use Constant Contact

<http://www.constantcontact.com> to host and manage our email lists, but other options are available. Using a third-party provider for e-mail will help you avoid issues with bandwidth overload on your host's email servers, and will keep you from having to deal with the hassle of blacklist management. (Many ISPs keep a "blacklist" of email servers that have sent their subscribers spam in the past. If your email server is hosted by an ISP on this list, your emails won't get through to certain subscribers.) Email-list management isn't cheap, though, and sometimes can cost you as much as your website hosting, should you get thousands of email subscribers.

☐ Design and print business cards

Sure, you're a paperless online business. But leaving behind these "old school" artifacts is helpful in building a network of clients, sources, customers and readers. Get your cards professionally printed, either using a local printer or an online service such as VistaPrint <http://www.vistaprint.com>. (Be careful when ordering from services such as VistaPrint, though, as they'll try to upsell you at what seems like every step of the ordering process.)

☐ Create a rate card

Potential advertisers will want to know how much you charge for their ads to appear on your site. So you'll need to establish (and publish) a rate card listing your available packages and prices. Get familiar with rate cards by looking at ones from other websites similar to yours. (Remember your assignment in Chapter 4?)

In Chapter 3, we talked about advertising revenue and the ways publishers price ads online — CPM [cost per thousand ad impressions], CPC [cost per click on an ad] and CPA [cost per action after clicking an ad — such as a commission on a sale]. If you're wondering about what size and format of ads to run on your site, the Internet Advertising Bureau [IAB] has established some industry standards for ad sizes:

<http://www.iab.net/guidelines/508676/508767/displayguidelines> If you're planning to sell rotating banner ads on your site, you should stick to the IAB standard ad sizes in your site templates. Based on my experience and talks with many other independent online publishers and advertisers, three of the IAB standard ad sizes stand out as most popular with advertisers:

- The 160-pixel-wide by 600-pixels-tall "Wide Skyscraper"
- The 729-pixels-wide by 90-pixels-tall "Leaderboard"
- The 300-pixels-wide by 250-pixels-tall "Medium Rectangle"

Using one or more of these ad sizes maximizes your earning potential from ad networks such as Google AdSense. If you'll be selling directly to advertisers who are placing campaigns on multiple websites, you'll find that these are the formats they're using most often. You'll increase your chances of closing a sale if a customer doesn't have to create a unique banner ad file for your site's non-standard ad sizes.

Where should you place the ads on your page design template? Google has researched that question and published an eye-tracking "heatmap" that shows where Internet users are most likely to look on various webpages:
<http://support.google.com/adsense/bin/answer.py?answer=1354747> Use Google's research and talk with other publishers on your action team to decide where to place your ads. Don't hesitate to experiment with ads in different locations, too. Collect data of your own and let that direct you to the optimal ad placement on your website.

On Violinist.com, we rotate ads into three positions on our pages and charge advertisers based on the number of impressions we deliver for their ads each month. Our rate card is public, so I'm happy to share it with you here (although I can't guarantee that we haven't changed it by the time you read this):

- $1,000 for 200,000 ad impressions in one month

- $750 for 150,000 ad impressions in one month
- $500 for 100,000 ad impressions in one month

If you do the math, you'll find that all four packages cost the same CPM — $5 for each 1,000 impressions. Over the years, we've found that price allows us to sell out our advertising inventory more months than not. When we first started selling ads, we set a CPM and let advertisers choose how many impression they wanted. That just confused advertisers and cost us sales. Now we just offer three, easy-to-understand price points. The more you pay, the more your ad gets seen. Simple.

So how did we decide what CPM to charge? And how did we figure out how many ad impressions we had available? Well, we'd been publishing the site for several years before we started selling our own ads, so we had years of traffic data to tell us how many impressions we'd have available. And we'd been serving Google AdSense ads on our site for at least a year before we started selling our own ads, so we knew what CPM revenue we were getting from those ads. Since we thought the guarantee of having ads on our site was worth something extra to our advertisers, we simply doubled the Google AdSense CPM and used that as our initial asking price for ads. Since then, we've changed the CPM price (many times!) to find the level where we are selling all of our ad inventory most months.

When you launch a new site, you can either use the "start with AdSense, then go from there with your own ads" method we used on Violinist.com, or you could simply sell fixed sponsorships to a couple of advertisers, until you have some reliable traffic data. Sell all of the impressions in a single ad position to one advertiser for a fixed price you both think is fair, then come up with your rate card once you see how many impressions and clicks that ad is delivering each month.

You can always change your rate card — but remember this: Advertising prices aren't set by your needs. They're set by what advertisers are willing to pay. No one cares what expenses you have or how much money you think you need to make this month. Advertisers will pay what they think is the market rate for your ads. Collect all the data you can to help you figure out what that market rate is and charge that. We'll talk more about data collection and analysis in Chapter 9.

☐ Create a media kit

You'll need to describe your site, on a single page, to convince readers to read it, advertisers to support it and other journalists to report about it. Start with the basics: the who, what, where, when and why about your new website. That's your initial media kit — a nicely designed, printed "one-pager" you can hand out to supporters and also post in HTML format on an "About Us" page on your website. Plan to update and expand your media kit as you gather more readership data, positive reviews from readers and testimonials from happy advertisers.

☐ Create a customer lead list

Whom will you solicit to become advertisers or funders for your website? That's your customer lead list. Gather contact information, then use your calendar to assign times to contact everyone on your list. And then assign yourself times to follow up by contacting them again if you haven't closed a sale or been rejected outright.

☐ Create a promotional lead list

Whom can you talk into writing about your site? At what events can you meet and recruit new readers? Where online can you promote the site, without looking like a spammer or scammer? List these promotional opportunities, then use your calendar to assign times to follow up on each opportunity.

> **EXERCISE**
>
> Sure, that's a pretty substantial to-do list. But before you read any further, I want to you to complete one of the items on that list.
>
> It's the customer lead list — the most valuable asset a start-up has. For your assignment, identify 20 potential customers in your community — people, businesses or organizations that might pay to support your publication. Write down a contact name, email, phone number and street address for each. Estimate what you think they would be willing to spend on your publication. You don't have to start contacting them yet (save that for when you go through this start-up checklist for real), but you should begin assembling this list right now. If you can't think of any potential customers for your publication, it's time to rethink your concept or the community you're intending to serve.

7 TIME TO MOBILIZE: DAILY REPORTING

The action plan helps you set up a website and the underlying business to support it. But empty shells of failed websites litter the Internet. To make your publication successful, you will need to keep it fresh with an ever-flowing stream of engaging content. Give up the illusion of "passive income." If you're going to make it in online publishing, you're going to have to mobilize and keep working. In the next two chapters, we'll talk about the reporting and presentation skills you will use on a daily basis in your publication.

If you're an experienced professional journalist, you might feel you can skip these chapters and start publishing. But I'd suggest you read these next two chapters anyway and that you do the exercises. The writing and reporting that you will be doing as an independent publisher might be quite different from the work you've been doing as a newspaper or broadcast employee. Make this a fresh start. Think of this as a basic exercise routine — one that refocuses on your core skills and keeps you in shape for the hard work you're about to do.

If you've not worked in the reporting business before, don't be intimidated. You'll discover that much of what you've done in your professional and personal lives applies to news publishing. After all, you've been collecting and passing along information all your life — from talking with friends in school to preparing reports for your boss. You've been reporting for years!

Four main elements make up almost all news reporting:

- Observation
- Interviews
- Looking at documents
- Analysis

Some journalists don't like the idea of including analysis as part of reporting. They see it as a different skill — one that's left to columnists and editorial writers. But one of the dirty secrets of journalism is that every reporter engages in analysis on every story she or he writes. Deciding whether to pursue a story requires analysis. Deciding whether a source is trustworthy enough to include in your reporting requires analysis. Deciding what to include in a story, and where, requires analysis.

Reporters do analysis all the time. So let's stop pretending otherwise. Let's instead acknowledge that analysis is part of the reporting process and learn how to do it well, to best ensure that the information we're giving our readers is accurate and truthful.

(Wondering about the difference between accurate and truthful? Here's an example. The following statement is accurate: "Bob Smith plunged his knife into the belly of the murder victim." Makes you think that Bob killed someone, right? Now let's add a little additional context. Try this statement, instead: "After being called into the Coroner's Office to help investigate another homicide, Dr. Bob Smith plunged his knife into the belly of the murder victim." Accurate reporting is never good enough. You want to strive for *truthful* reporting — information that's not only accurate but also that includes all the necessary context a reader needs to know the truth about the story.)

But before you can analyze information, you must collect it. Let's start there.

Observation

When I refer to your observations, I don't mean your opinions or conclusions about things. I mean the things you see, hear, touch, smell and taste with your five senses. Observation in a reporting context is purely factual — sensory input, alone.

Want an example? Sit on a park bench for an hour. What do you see? You might be tempted to think of observation as passive information collection, but good observation requires an active decision to pay close attention to details. You've got to stay engaged with what you're seeing, hearing, touching, smelling and tasting, if you want to be able to retell the information you collect in a way that will engage your readers.

What are you seeing from your park bench? Do you feel a breeze? What's the food cooking on that grill over there smell like? Can you hear what the people next to the grill are saying? Watch their body language. What about that couple on the footpath over there? Let your eyes follow them for a while. Do they tell you a story? Notice the bird, flying to and from the tree top above you. What is it up to?

Simply record every detail you observe. Don't censor yourself while taking notes. Force yourself you to see the things life might have conditioned you to ignore. If you see someone peeing behind a building, don't look away. In your reporter mode, you need to write that down.

While you don't want to censor your observations, you should turn off your imagination while reporting. You don't need to use your imagination for any of this, and you shouldn't. Don't make up anything. Don't fill in a single blank. If you pay close attention and record enough detail, these items will provide you the building blocks of a narrative when you start writing later. You won't need to spin a fictional narrative to keep your readers' attention.

The ultimate observation exercise for a writer might be the restaurant review. There's no one to interview, no documents to examine (save the menu and the check at the end of the meal). It's just you and the food, brought to the reader by your ability to describe it.

Start with entering the restaurant — the surrounding neighborhood, the entrance, the wait for your table. What do you see, smell, hear as you walk to your seat? How does the chair and your table feel as you sit? The menu, as you hold it in your hands? The weight of the silverware and glasses? Note the selections on the menu. (I snap a picture. Cell phone photos are provide a great, modern way to "take notes" on printed material such as restaurant menus.) How long until your food arrives? You might not use all this information in your review, but you need to note it. You won't know what the story is until the meal's over. Make note of everything up until that moment, so you have it to use if you need it.

When the food arrives, note how it looks and smells, even how it feels as it sits in front of you. Can you feel a change in temperature? Great reviews don't tell you whether something is "good" or "bad" — who knows what a writer means with such vague language? The best reviews bring you to a scene, describing it in such vivid detail that you feel yourself experiencing the same moment.

So as you record your observations, leave out all analysis and evaluation. Don't write whether something tastes good or bad. Describe *how* it tastes, comparing it with other experiences you've had. (And that your audience likely has had, as well.)

Obviously, the more experiences you've had, the easier it will be for you to make these comparisons. It's much easier to describe the taste of a meal if you know the tastes of thousands of individual ingredients. (Just as it's easier to describe that scene in the park if you know the names of all the trees, bushes, flowers and grasses there.) But don't forget that it's your readers' knowledge and experiences that matter more than your own. To communicate effectively, you need to describe a scene in a way that your readers will understand. Talking about the taste of cardamon or the smell of bougainvillea does nothing if your readers have no clue what they are. That's why it's so important for writers to be part of the communities they cover — so that they have those shared experiences and common reference points that make it easier for the writer to describe new things in ways his or her readers immediately will understand.

Use observation to supplement your reporting in every story. When you are interviewing someone, observations can help provide telling details a reader can't find in a transcript. Any detail that helps a reader feel as though he or she is with you in a scene helps engage that reader in your story. But if you don't pay close attention to the details surrounding you as you report, you won't have those golden nuggets of information to entice your readers to stay with you.

Looking at Documents

When I first learned news reporting, in the pre-Web era, document searches typically required a trip to the local courthouse, getting on the good side of a clerk or secretary and paging through file cabinets or bound records. Today, searching documents is almost always done online. It can be a simple as calling up the right website.

Of course, the trick is to find that correct website. And not all the great unpublished stories and blog posts are waiting for you online. You'll still need to make that trip to the courthouse or city hall for many local records or for older records that have not been digitized and placed online.

Here are some sources of public documents I've used for stories in the past:

The United States Census Bureau <http://www.census.gov> — Check your community's population, income and demographic changes from year to year. These changes foretell just about every other story that will happen in your community, from retail stores opening or closing, school test scores going up or down, how much the government will collect and spend, and even the mix of cuisines served in the restaurants you'll see around town.

Trademark applications <http://www.uspto.gov/trademarks> — The single best place to find out about new products from companies you cover is the U.S. Patent and Trademark Office. Here's where you can search companies' new trademark applications, which will tell you the names of those new products before they go public. I frequently search the trademark database when reporting for ThemeParkInsider.com, to find the names of new rides and shows that companies such as Disney and Universal are planning for their theme parks.

Corporate reports <http://www.sec.gov/edgar/searchedgar/webusers.htm> — All publicly traded corporations in the United States are required to file regular reports with the U.S. Securities and Exchange Commission, which makes them available to the public through its EDGAR website. In these annual and quarterly reports, you'll find information about what companies are earning, where they're spending their money, how much they're paying top executives, and what contracts and deals they are making with other businesses and governments.

Federal legislation <http://thomas.loc.gov> — The Library of Congress' Thomas website offers the complete text of every bill before Congress and well as legislation from past sessions of

Congress. It's not common practice in online journalism, but I believe that whenever you write about a bill, you should mention its bill number and hyperlink that to its full text on Thomas. Why not let your readers who want more information about a bill see the whole thing for themselves? Most states also offer the full text of pending legislation on their state websites. Hyperlink those local bills, too, whenever you have the chance.

Campaign contributions <http://www.opensecrets.org> and <http://www.fec.gov/pindex.shtml> — The most important information you can give your readers during a political campaign is to show them who's giving money to the candidates and causes on their ballot. Forget what candidates say. The greatest predictor of what a candidate actually *will do* once elected is found in who's paying for the candidate's campaign. The Federal Election Commission collects and records contributions to candidates for federal office — President, Senate and the House of Representatives. The Center for Responsive Politics' OpenSecrets.org website offers another interface to search the FEC data, one that many reporters find easier to use. Most states also report contributions to state and local campaigns through their Secretary of State's website. Look for the one in your state to report on local races.

Crime reports <https://www.crimereports.com> and <http://www.fbi.gov/about-us/cjis/ucr/ucr> — CrimeReports.com collects incident reports from local law enforcement agencies and maps them in a convenient interface, but the data tend to be a few days' old, so it's not always the best source for a breaking news publication. The FBI's Uniform Crime Reports are the definitive source for crime data in the United States, and a great source when you're reporting a story on crime trends nationwide or for a state or metropolitan area. Still, if you want breaking crime news, the best sources are your local police officers and sheriff's deputies. Get to know their PIOs [public information officers] and learn their procedures for releasing information to the public (i.e. you).

Health data <*http://www.cdc.gov/nchs/fastats*> — The Center for Disease Control and Prevention's FastStats provides data on the number of incidents in the United States of just about every disease and health issue imaginable. It's a great source to provide needed context whenever you write a health story.

Zoning and building permits *(check local sources)* — Want to know what new businesses are opening in your town? Want to know what new housing developments are coming? Your local planning commission will have that information first, as developers file for zoning variances and/or building permits. As much as business people sometimes try to keep their developments secret until they're ready to open, there's no hiding from the planning commission. Their filings and applications are public records, so get to know the people in the office and when the commission meets, and you'll have a steady stream of news posts that curious local readers will want to see.

Above all, when searching public documents remember truthfulness — if you can get documents from one source and not from another, acknowledge that. Don't write a story based on public records as though other sources don't exist. It's a cheap shot, for example, to write a story on salaries of public employees if you don't include data on what local private sector employees with similar skills and experience earn, for context.

Interviews

When you can't find the information you need through observation or looking at documents, you'll need to ask someone. That's interviewing. Interviews can provide quick nuggets of information to supplement a post, or they can become features unto themselves — in-depth conversations with interesting people.

Unless I'm covering a breaking news situation and talking with eyewitnesses, I never conduct an interview without doing a document search first. At the very least, you want to know some information about the person with whom you're speaking, so that you come into the interview with questions likely to elicit informed, thoughtful answers. A Google search or other background check will help you know that you've selected a source with some knowledge and experience on your topic.

Once you've decided whom to interview, you'll need to decide how to conduct the interview. Interviews can be conducted:

- In person
- Via video calls
- Over the phone
- Via email
- Via online text chat

In-person interviews allow you to use your observation skills while you do the interview. You can watch how a person reacts to your questions and observe the surroundings, all while getting the answers to your questions. You can read body language, and if you are doing the interview in the subject's home or office, you can ask questions about things you see there — opportunities you would have missed if you'd done the interview over the phone or by email. Physically expressive people often use their hands and bodies in conversation, and being there in person allows you to better describe those individuals to your readers. In-person interviews also allow you to capture high-quality video of your subject — essential if you're preparing a video report. But if a subject doesn't live near you, traveling to meet him or her can cost a lot of time and money.

A video chat allows you observation opportunities, though you won't be able to see things outside the camera's view. That's still better than being limited to a voice conversation. Video chats can be conducted now at little or no cost, allowing for the option of a "next best thing" to in-person interviews for reporters pressed for time or with a limited budget. Video quality is getting better, too, and now even some broadcast television stations use video calls for on-air interviews with subjects in a different city. (Skype <http://www.skype.com> provides a popular option for free video calling.)

Phone calls have the advantage of immediacy, relatively low cost, and the ability to follow-up with additional questions. You will need a hands-free phone for note-taking, and additional equipment if you want to record calls (which can be tricky on many models of cell phones). And, of course, both you and you subject have to be available at the same time, or you'll find yourself in a dreaded game of "phone tag." When you connect, make sure that both you and your source have a good-quality connection so you can complete the interview uninterrupted — without a dropped call or interference.

Texting also allows you to contact a source immediately, and many sources will respond to texts before they return phone calls. Questions and answers have to be short, though, so this is often a better medium for quick questions than in-depth interviews.

Email is asynchronous — which is bad if you're on a deadline, but great if you're trying to get answers from a source on the other side of the world. It's a written medium, so it's often the best way to conduct an interview with fellow writers, who communicate best with the written word and might not be as articulate when they speak. With an email interview, you won't need to transcribe answers from an audio recording or your notes — it's as easy and copying and pasting your sources' responses into your story. Be careful, though, for in an email interview it's easy for a source to paste canned answers from a spokesperson instead of speaking for herself or himself. If you're interviewing a politician or business person who often hides behind a PR staff, you'll want to conduct the interview in a different medium to ensure you're getting your source's own words.

If you are recording video or audio of your source, such as

over a phone call, many states require you to get your source's explicit permission, otherwise you could be breaking local laws against wiretapping. Best practice is to start the recording and immediately to ask the source for their permission to record, so that you have his or her approval on the recording before you move onto any other questions.

And do ask questions in your interview. Don't just make a statement, then sit there in silence, waiting for your source to respond. That's the surest way to end up with an awkward interview — with your source stammering, trying to figure out what he or she is "supposed" to say to you.

Most sources will try to guess what you want, and give you the answers they think you're looking for. Your job is to get past that, and to get a comfortable conversation flowing, so the source instead will share with you the personal experiences and expertise that you really want.

Begin at the beginning. When my wife is interviewing violinists, she always starts by asking them when they began playing the violin, and why they decided to start playing. From there, they can begin a conversation about the development of that violinist's career, leading up to whatever project they're currently on. By doing this, she's getting the background and context that will allow her to write a more engaging story about the project. It's always better to have more information than you need for a story than not enough.

Don't limit yourself to questions that can be answered with a yes or no. And don't ask people for their opinions. No one cares about anyone else's opinion about anything. Ask instead for people to describe their experiences. Ask them to explain why and how they know whatever it is you're asking them about. When you are interviewing, *you are asking your source to be the reporter.* You are asking them to report back to you the observations and evidence that they've found from other sources, over the course of their life and their work. You have a right to insist that they stick to the facts, too. Your readers will thank you for that with their continued attention if you do.

And if don't understand completely what a source is reporting to you, you'll never be able to turn around and explain it to your readers. Don't be afraid to ask your source to explain something again. I often say something along the lines of "I'm struggling with how I'm going to describe this to my readers so they understand it. Could you explain that again?" to a source, to try to elicit a clearer description.

I always record every interview I do that isn't done via email or text. I'll take written notes during the interview to note something significant and the time mark when the source said it, for reference when I'm transcribing the interview. (Some reporters transcribe their entire interview before writing a piece. I typically write the piece in my head instead as I listen to the recording, and transcribe only the quotes I'm planning to use.) It's been years since I met a beginning reporter who used hand-written shorthand to take notes in an interview instead of just making a recording. But that is an option if you know how to use shorthand.

If you are planning to record an interview for broadcast, whether it be an audio podcast or a video report, it's best to do a "pre-interview" with the source, so that he or she knows the gist of the interview and begins preparing thoughtful answers. A pre-interview also helps you to have an idea what lines of questioning are likely to elicit the most engaging answers. The last thing you want in a broadcast interview is "dead air," while the source searches for the right thing to say. Prepare with a pre-interview and you can save yourself a lot of editing time later, when you'd have to cut all the boring and useless parts of the interview.

Analysis

Once you've gathered your information, it's time to decide what information will make it into your story and what won't. To make that decision, let's go back to what we learned in Chapter 1: The most important thing you do as a publisher is to find a need and meet it. So think about your readers. What information do they need? What do they want? Use the answers to those questions to guide you when deciding what reporting to pursue and what to include from your reporting in your stories.

Ultimately, your reporting should do two things: Spread truthful information and debunk untruthful information. Quoting a source who is lying, without debunking those lies, is as bad as lying yourself. Your job isn't to be a stenographer, faithfully transcribing whatever a source wants you to say. Your job is to take the information you can collect, analyze it and present it to your readers. Present them information that meets their needs. (If you truly are an expert about your community, you will find information your readers didn't know yet that they need.) Skip irrelevant information. Because if you don't, your readers will — by ignoring you.

The Internet floods your audience with information. People need publishers who can reliably filter it into truthful, relevant, engaging (and even sometimes entertaining) reports, without distracting them with any misleading garbage.

How will you do that? First, read your own writing. Does it make sense to you? Are there any logical flaws, missing pieces, details that just don't fit? If so, report more. Find the missing pieces. Find the credible source who can explain things. Find another angle from which to look at the details so they all line up.

Here's an example: Reporters and political candidates were hammering my children's public school district in the local paper. Even though the district's average test scores were going up from year to year, they remained below the state's average. To the politicians, this meant that the district was failing and the community needed to clean house — new school board members, charter schools, and more cuts to the district's budget. (I still don't understand how cutting a school district budget is supposed to help students learn more and score better on standardize tests.)

I wanted to know *why* the district's scores were lagging the state average. I knew that my kids were getting a good education in their schools — they posted high scores on those tests every year. Their friends were scoring above average as well. Where were the kids who were scoring so poorly?

I decided to do some analysis. I went to the California state website that publishes school and district test scores <http://star.cde.ca.gov>. Instead of just looking at the top-line score for the district as a whole, I decided to look at the various subgroups — breaking down the student population by ethnicity and economic status.

I started by looking at my family's category — white students who were not "economically disadvantaged." (In education statistics, "economically disadvantaged" means students whose family income is low enough that they qualify for the federal government's free or reduced-price school lunch program — that was about $41,000 a year for a family of four in California in 2012.) In my family's category, I found that students in my kids' school district scored far above the state average for other white, non-disadvantaged students.

So that's not where the problem was. As far as kids like mine were concerned, they were attending an above-average school district. Next, I looked at white, economically disadvantaged students. There weren't as many, but still, the local students beat the state average in their category.

Then I looked at Latino and African-American students. No matter what category I looked at, economically disadvantaged or not, the students in my local school district were beating the state average for students in that same ethnic or economic category. So where the heck were the below-average students, the ones bringing down the district's scores?

That's when I remembered that the average scores for the

students in the "economically disadvantaged" categories fell far below the average scores for students whose families didn't qualify for free or reduced-price school lunch. And in our local school district, we had *way* more economically disadvantaged students than the state average — more than 70 percent of the students in the district qualified for free or reduced-price lunches.

The problem wasn't that the schools were failing. In fact, the schools were succeeding. The poor students were scoring above the state average for poor students. The middle-class and wealthy students were scoring above the state average for middle-class and wealthy students. The problem was that we had so many more poor kids than the state average. Since poor students scored so much lower on state tests, that pulled the district's overall test scores below the state's average test scores for all students.

That analysis changes the narrative. No longer is this a story about a school district failing to educate its students. Now this is a story about child poverty and about how rising poverty overwhelms schools' ability to close the achievement gap created by families that can't make ends meet. It's not just the lack of money for lunch. It's usually a lack of money for books in the home, a quiet place to study, English-speaking, educated parents to help with homework, and even giving a kid a bed to sleep in, in some cases. And forget about the outside music lessons, club sports and tutoring help that middle-class and wealthy students enjoy.

If I simply quoted the same critics the local newspaper did, I'd have missed the real story and mislead my readers as a result. This is just one example of why informed analysis isn't optional for news reporters — it's an essential part of the job.

If you're concerned about your ability to use math to analyze data your collect, don't be. In the appendix to this book, you'll find several easy-to-read lessons in basic statistics that I've written to help even the most math-phobic writers understand and use basic statistics. I've included a lesson in the difference between "mean" and "median," and when to use each in a story. Another shows how to figure out percentages and rates of change. Good math also can help you better understand public opinion polls, so I've described the concept of "margin of error." Skip back to that section whenever you have a question about using math in a news story and to find a few more story ideas, too.

If you're still uncomfortable analyzing a story, don't be afraid to admit it. Journalists make a grave mistake when they pretend they know everything. Media critic and former newspaper columnist Dan Gillmor wrote in the introduction of his book *We the Media*, "my readers know more than I do." Make this your attitude, too. Collectively, your readers have more information about any given topic than you could ever hope to collect. Invite them to become part of your reporting and analysis, instead of shutting them out. Ask them for tips, leads and advice when you need them. Explain to them how and why you collected and presented the information in your stories and give them the opportunity to comment.

You want your readers not to feel like they're outsiders looking in, but companions who are working with you in the process of discovering more about their community. We'll talk more about writing styles in the next chapter, but engaging your readers in your work can pay off with richer and more accurate reporting and analysis. It also can help you build a larger, more loyal audience.

EXERCISES

We've got two assignments for you in this chapter.

Observation: Sit in a public place in your community for one hour, and then write a story about what you observed. You can take notes, but do not interview anyone. Don't place yourself in the story. And don't fill in the gaps by assuming, presuming or making up anything to explain what you see, hear, feel, etc. Craft a strictly factual observation of your hour, but try to make it as engaging a narrative as you can in 750-1,000 words.

Data collection and analysis: Who were the biggest contributors to election campaigns in your zip code? For the most recent federal election cycle, go online and find contribution data for Congressional and Presidential campaigns from people in your zip code. Which parties and candidates received the most money? Which had the most contributors? (Those aren't always the same.) Tell the most interesting and engaging story you can with that data in 1,000-1,250 words.

8 IMPLEMENT THE ACTION WITH PRESENTATION SKILLS

The simplest form of online publishing is blogging: describe what you're covering in words and post it. But as an online publisher, you have many more options for communicating the information you believe will meet your audience's needs. You can use photos, video, audio podcasts, the give-and-take of a discussion forum — even apps, games and eBooks if you want to look beyond the traditional Web. Part of your daily decision will be not just *what* to cover, but *how* to present it.

In this chapter, we'll talk about how best to present the information you've collected for your audience. We'll start with traditional forms — writing, speaking, photography, video. Then we'll address how to conduct yourself as a public person online, using social media to strengthen your publication business while avoiding the dangers of having social media hurt or destroy your credibility as a publisher.

Writing

Text remains the backbone of Internet content. Great writing can distinguish your site from the millions of others that clog the search engines and compete for your readers' time and attention. No matter how much (or how little) experience you have writing for others, you can write posts that people will want to read.

Shinichi Suzuki, the creator of the Suzuki Method of music instruction, said that a student needed to practice a task 10,000 times in order to master it. So it is with writing. The sooner you start on your 10,000 articles, the sooner you will master the skill of writing. If you're not already in the habit of writing every day, start by keeping a journal. That's why I asked you to put all of your exercise assignments in one place — to start a habit of collecting your thoughts and work in the same place, on a regular basis.

(At one of our OJR conferences, former Slashdot editor Robin "Roblimo" Miller shared a great line about why Slashdot called its reader-submitted content "journals" instead of "blogs." He said: "If a person who keeps a blog is a 'blogger', then a person who keeps a journal is a...?" That line always makes me smile whenever some frustrated newspaper writer tries to start another "bloggers aren't journalists" flame war.)

As important as daily writing is to building your skills, you'll become an even better writer through reading. Make reading a daily habit, too. And be sure to read more than just news stories and other blog entries. Read books, long magazine articles and poetry. Read great writers and notice what they do with their words. Pay attention to sentence length, verb tenses and vocabulary. Notice how they set a scene, introduce characters and then how they move the action through conversation versus moving it through exposition.

Then contrast what you've learned from those authors with what you see in daily news reports, in papers and online. How does that writing differ? What would you do to make those stories better?

Notice what writing grabs you and demands your attention. What could you do to write like that?

Then go practice in your journal.

Use reporting exercises to stretch your writing "muscles." Go sit in a park for a while and write about it — just as I asked you to do in that observation exercise in the previous chapter. Interview people and tell their stories. Eventually, your needs as a writer will force you to improve as a reporter, to gather better building blocks of information you'll need to construct more engaging stories.

Pulitzer Prize winner Jon Franklin wrote in his book *Writing for Story* that all great stories can be reduced to a simple formula: a conflict, followed by a resolution. Political activist Markos Moulitsas, founder of the website Daily Kos, wrote in *Taking on the System* that authors engage readers by framing stories with heroes and villains. So when you fire up your computer to write, think about those roles. What's the conflict in your story? Is there a resolution? Who's the hero, trying to find the good resolution? Who (or what) is the villain, standing in the way?

Not every story you'll write will require epic construction. Sometimes the "conflict" is pretty simple — people don't know that Walt Disney World has opened a new website for people to make restaurant reservations. The resolution is that you'll tell them, and link the URL, in a short blog post. That's it. You'll fulfilled an audience need. Good job.

No matter how short and simply you aim to write, great writing demands sharp editing. When you look back at the information you've collected, ask yourself, "What can I tell my readers here that will actually help them in some way?" Always remember, you are publishing to serve your readers. If the information you've collected won't help your readers in any meaningful way, don't waste their time. Leave it out.

Mix up your work to help keep your readers' attention. Don't keep writing the same things in the same way. Rob Malda, another former Slashdot editor, compared that website to an omelette. The idea, he wrote, was to get a tasty mix of different ingredients on the page each day. That can be a mix of topics you cover, as well as mix of different types of posts. Perhaps your "omelette" will include a mix of interesting links, news updates, interviews, profiles and investigative pieces. Or your mix might include short posts, long essays, video clips and discussions with readers. Look for the mix that engages your audience and keeps people clicking to you.

Ultimately, your audience will decide what flavors they want in their omelette. But you'll improve your writing if you remain mindful of conflict and resolution, and of heroes and villains, whenever you write. Look for opportunities to tell longer stories that engage readers with stories of heroes seeking resolutions and fighting villains who stand in their way. Don't force those roles when your reporting won't support them. But don't cheat your readers by hiding those great narratives when the reporting is there.

Whatever you're writing, think of a reader. Imagine yourself talking with him or her. You don't want your words to come across as the work of a faceless institution, the words of an anonymous committee of hacks. People respond better to friendly individuals than they do to corporate drones. That's why so many companies give their employees nametags. They want you to see them as individuals, so you'll feel better dealing with them.

So however or whatever you write, it should sound like *you*. Don't try to write "fancy" — just tell the story. Don't try to imitate anyone or anything else, especially a writer at one of those newspapers millions of people have stopped reading. You have to feel comfortable with what you write, so that your audience will feel comfortable reading it. That comes with practice — your 10,000 attempts.

Consider not just your words, but how they'll look on your site, too. When I first started publishing online in the 1990s, we had to use sans-serif typefaces in our site designs to make our words readable on the low-resolution computer screens of the time. Now, with retina displays and other high-resolution screens widely available, you can choose from a wider selection of serif and sans-serif typefaces to get the look and readability you want for your site.

Use bullet-point lists, blockquotes and bolded text, when appropriate, to break up the flow of text on your page. Many readers scan a page before committing to read it. If you can use these typographical elements to make major points "pop" from the text on a quick visual scan, you increase the chance of hooking a visitor into sticking with the page and reading the full article. Dense, gray text begs a reader to click on to someone else's site. Let me refer you back to Shay Howe's excellent primer on HTML <*http://learn.shayhowe.com/html-css*> for more advice on how to make your writing look engaging and accessible online, without sacrificing function.

Don't worry about search engine optimization [SEO]. Just write using the words and phrases that you believe other people will use when searching for stories on a particular topic. Those are the words and phrases you should be using in your headlines and first paragraphs of your posts. If you use them, the search engine traffic will find you. Don't waste time trying to game the system. That's for people who can't write clear, compelling stories.

If you want to attract more traffic via search engines, try writing FAQ [answers to frequently asked questions] pages on the most popular topics you will cover — one page per topic. You can use these pages to link to your top stories on these topics, in addition to providing a clearly-written, easy-to-read summary of the topic on the page itself.

> **EXERCISE**
>
> Writers build great stories with nouns and verbs. You can flirt with an adjective now and then, but stop writing and smack yourself in the face before you use an adverb. If you use state-of-being words — "is," "are," "am," "was," "been," "be," or "being" — as your verb, try rewriting the sentence using a more active verb. Use "active voice" — verbs without a subject (known as "passive voice") belong only in legal stories where "a crime has been committed," but no one's legally declared whodunit yet.
>
> For your exercise, pick three short news stories or blog posts from other websites. First, find the verb in every sentence of each post. Then rewrite the each story, eliminating state-of-being verbs and passive voice. Kill the adverbs, too. Can you do it? Can you write a better version of these stories than their authors did? Give it a try. This exercise will prepare you for editing your own work, after you've launched your site.

Speaking

Strong speaking skills will allow you engage additional visitors through audio podcasts and video clips. You'll also need to speak well to recruit new readers and action team members through personal meetings, public events and appearances on others' radio, TV and online shows. I've promoted my websites in interviews on NPR, the BBC, CNN and the CBS Evening News. The better you can speak naturally while telling engaging stories about your site and your community, the more promotional opportunities you'll find available to you. So get in front of the mirror and practice.

Not every visitor prefers to get information through reading text. Many visitors prefer to listen, instead. They love to buy audiobooks and download podcasts. They listen to the Web through earphones at work, while the boss sees spreadsheets and department reports on their computer screens. If you can't deliver information in the way these visitors want it, you'll lose them — and the advertisers and funders who want to reach them.

How can you become a better public speaker? Start by applying your writing skills. Don't ever "wing it" it public — have at least a plan, if not a script that you've written in advance. Then memorize it. Practice in front of mirror — or better, video-record yourself — to see how you'll look to an audience. If you're going to be interviewed, try to anticipate the questions, then prepare answers for them.

Almost all broadcasters will "pre-interview" potential guests before they appear on the show, so both you and the host will know what the other is likely to say. No host wants to broadcast "dead air" or a confused and verbally stumbling guest. (For radio and television shows, pre-interviews are almost always done by someone other than the show host. Online, where we don't always have co-workers, most people do their own pre-interviews. If you're planning to interview guests for a podcast or video report, use a pre-interview with that guest to help you craft a more professional-quality show. You don't need to reveal every question you're going to ask, particularly if you've got a question to which you don't want a prepared response. But you should *always* go over the mechanics of your specific interview process with a guest before recording.)

When speaking, I've got three rules:

- **Keep it simple, but never stupid.** Theme park fans and violinists — like most niche communities — have their own special languages of jargon and acronyms. Bar them from your script when you're speaking to an outside audience. I don't recommend trying to "speak down" to an audience. Assume that your audience is knowledgeable and interested — just don't use any "insider" jargon or language. Simply use plain English — commonly used words and phrases — to express what you want to say.

- **Slow down, but don't stumble.** Inexperienced public speakers often rush when they speak. Too-fast talk leaves your audience feeling stressed, even if they can understand what you're saying. Poor speakers then overreact to their haste by stopping suddenly during their talk, stumbling over words, as they try to get back to what they wanted to say. Practice speaking — slow and steady, with intentional pauses, inflection and changes in volume — to nail your performance.

- **Appeal to emotion, but don't get emotional.** A good talk gets your audience thinking. A *great* talk hits 'em in the heart, as well. You don't want your audience just thinking about your words. You want to inspire them to action, as well. You can do that by telling a story, sharing an anecdote or asking a question that elicits emotion from your listeners. Emotion primes reaction. You don't help yourself if *you're* the one showing the emotion, though. That just shifts attention back to you. You want the audience engaged with your words and their own reaction to them — not thinking about you as some performer.

If you're appearing on camera or in person, consider your body language when speaking, too. In his book *The Presentation Secrets of Steve Jobs: How to Be Insanely Great in Front of Any Audience*, author Carmine Gallo offered some great tips for improving your body language.

- **Eye Contact:** Looking your audience in the eye shows your interest in them as individuals. For broadcast appearances, look at the camera — not the monitor, if you're speaking with a host in another studio. (If you're in the same studio or location as the host, go ahead and look him or her in the eye and don't worry about the camera.)

- **Open Posture:** Place nothing between you and the audience, such as a lectern. Keep your body square, facing the people you're addressing. Don't turn to the side, turn your back, cross your arms, or hold anything that separates you from them. You want to look engaged, accessible and friendly. Turning away or hiding behind something shows you're not interested in your audience, which will lead them to become less interested in you. If you're demonstrating something, hold it to your side so that you can remain angled toward the audience and they can see what you're doing.

- **Hand Gestures:** Disciplined hand gestures can help your audience better understand what you're saying, as they can emphasize important points. Be careful, though, because thoughtless hand gestures distract the audience and undercut your presentation. On camera, limit your hand gestures to the baseball "strike zone" — the rectangle between your chest and waist, not extending beyond the sides of your body. That's a pretty small area, but it's all you'll need. On stage, you can extend your hands and arms outside the "strike zone," but only when you want to make a *very* dramatic point. However you use hand gestures, script them before you speak, as you do your words.

When appearing on stage (or anywhere in front of an audience where you can move around), walk around the stage only to emphasize a transition between points in your speech. Keep your feet still and use your hands when you want to emphasize a point.

Finally, learn to purge your words of annoying verbal ticks, such as "um...," "you know...," and "like...". Gallo suggested asking a friend to watch you speak, and asking her to tap a water glass with a spoon, or something else, whenever you interject one of these annoyances into your speech. It's basic, Pavlovian conditioning — use some annoying stimulus to make you aware of when you do something wrong, to help you break that habit.

> **EXERCISE**
>
> Haul out the video camera (a smartphone camera will do) and either ask someone to record you, or record yourself, giving your pitch speech (from Chapter 1). Watch the video and examine your speech, your cadence, your tone and your body language. Can you do better? Keep recording takes until you've nailed it. Then save that video for use in your online "media kit." (Remember that? From the checklist in Chapter 6?)

Photography

Here's another hard-learned lesson, one I realized after several years of online publishing: To maximize traffic, you *must* include a photograph in every blog entry or article you post. And you don't want to resort to posting the same stock photos one can find on thousands of other webpages, either. That won't help your posts stand out from the crowd. You need to learn how to take and publish engaging photographs if you're to earn a viable audience online.

I'll admit it — I'm cheap. I believe in the no-cost start-up, launching a website business by spending as little money as possible. You don't have to go out and spend several hundred dollars on a digital SLR camera if you've got a cell phone or a "point & shoot" that takes decent-enough pictures. Website display resolution remains low enough on most screens and devices that a well-composed camera-phone picture will look good online, provided you keep the image size relatively small (under 500 pixels wide or tall). But a professional quality DSLR, from Canon, Nikon or Olympus, takes pictures at a far higher resolution that you'll ever get from even the latest iPhone or Android phone. If you really want to wow readers with your photos, or run large images on your site, a digital SLR will repay your investments in buying and learning how to use it.

But you don't absolutely have to have one to launch your site. What you *do* have to do, though, is **learn how to take a picture *in focus*.** Blurry images scream "I'm an amateur!" as loudly as publishing your site in a Comic Sans font, with a star-field background and animated-GIF cats in the margins. Whether you use "tap to focus" on a phone or aim your camera at its subject to trigger the auto-focus on a point & shoot, make sure you know how to engage your camera's focus properly to get a sharp picture.

Once you know how to focus your shots, think about their composition to ensure that you're shooting photos your readers will notice. After focusing, the next-best rule for photography is ***get close to your subject***. You want the subject of your photo to fill the frame. You've got too little space on the screen to waste any pixels on unnecessary background. You can use the zoom to close in on your subject, but just walking in as close as you can is the best way to preserve the highest possible resolution for your shot.

What subjects work best in a photo? Try these:

- **Emotional faces.** People respond best to faces, especially ones expressing some emotion. (And not just human faces, either. There's a reason why LOL Cats became one of the Internet's hottest memes. People project emotion onto animal faces, too.) These pictures literally "put a face" on your story, making it more emotionally accessible to readers. Again, get in close or use your zoom (or crop the image on your computer later), so that the face you focus on fills the image to make it most powerful.

- **Beautiful scenery.** Drop-dead, gorgeous images of beautiful landscapes, buildings or artworks can keep readers clicking on your website for hours. Whether it's a shot of the castle at Tokyo Disneyland or the detail on the tailpiece of a Stradivarius violin, keep the composition tight to maximize the visual impact of the shot. Don't forget to find the beauty in small things, too. My son spent an afternoon at school once taking stunning photos of leaves and puddles after a rare Southern California rainstorm. Get close, focus on your subject and shoot away.

- **Dramatic lighting**. This is less a subject for a photo than an important element of a great shot. Bad lighting kills photos almost as much as blurry focus. Warm, natural sunlight is your best friend — provided you keep it behind you so it illuminates the subject you're shooting. Once you get some experience with photography, try shooting contrasts of light and shadow for dramatic effect. (A person emerging from a shadow can provide a stunning photo.) Digital SLRs show their worth in low-light situations, where they can find resolution that's lost when using cheaper cameras. If you're taking a picture indoors, try to position the shot so you've got open windows behind you, to light your subject more naturally. If you need to use artificial light to illuminate your subject indoors, try to make it indirect to recreate the effect of warm, natural sunlight. That's why pro photographers use light shields or bounce flashes off white pieces of cardboard and such.

Once you've shot your photos, prepare them for publication using a photo editing tool such as Photoshop. That's the industry leader, but you can find much more affordable alternatives such as Photoshop Express, Pixelmator and Aperture. Heck, my Macbook's image Preview tool can crop, resize and do basic color correction on photographs. If you've set up your shot well, that might be all you need.

"Wild art" photos can stand alone as a blog post or Facebook page filler on a slow news day. I've taken more than 5,000 photos of theme park attractions over the years — rides, shows and even theme park meals. Every once in a while, I'll drop one of those into a post, usually by itself, and I'm never surprised when that single-photo post ends up eliciting the most comments and Facebook "Likes" of any post that week. I know that if I upload a crisp shot of a sugar-dusted Monte Cristo sandwich from Disneyland to my Facebook page or Pinterest account, I'm good for hundreds of clicks, Likes and Shares. People love great photographs.

With solid photo skills, you've got no excuse for failing to maintain a regular publishing schedule. Whatever is (or is not) going on in your community, you always can find a great photo to take.

> **EXERCISE**
>
> Let's start building your library of go-to community photos. Your assignment is to take 100 new photos. You can photograph anything — but you should apply the principles I've described above. Get out of the house and use this exercise as an excuse to further explore the community you want to cover.

Video

I strongly suggest posting all your publication's videos to YouTube, both to save on bandwidth costs and to take advantage of YouTube's large user base and potential as a viral marketing network. Video files take up a huge amount of space on a computer

— hundreds of megabytes of space for just seconds of video. Many hosting providers charge by how much space your publication takes up on its computers. In addition, they'll charge you for the amount of data they deliver to readers requesting pages and files from your website. A single viral video, hosted on your site, can drive your traffic way past your hosting plan's maximum data transfer level for the month. That potentially can leave your site offline — or it can leave you facing an excess bandwidth charge that could set you back tens of thousands of dollars.

Avoid that disaster by uploading your videos to YouTube and embedding them into your blog posts and articles. According to 2012 data, YouTube's search function is the second-most-used search engine on the Internet, following its corporate parent, Google. YouTube has become the default search engine for video on the Web. If you want your videos to be seen widely, they need to be there.

I've worked with filmmakers who swear by Vimeo, a competing video hub that earned buzz early on for featuring higher-resolution video display than YouTube did. Today, Vimeo attracts a niche crowd, with a community that's far more supportive of creative filmmaking than YouTube's. But if you're looking for views, instead of affirmation, you should choose the far more popular YouTube platform instead.

Vimeo fans have one great point, though — YouTube's comment community stinks like an open landfill on a hot summer day. Protect your dignity, and your sanity, by changing the default settings on each video you upload, to allow comments only after you approve them. That will keep the worst of YouTube's foul-mouthed trolls from polluting your video pages while allowing reasonable comments through.

The same rules of focus, lighting and composition you learned for still photos apply to video, too. But you have another element to consider — motion. Your goal in shooting video should be to move your camera as little as possible. Your camera is your readers' eyes. Move it too much, and your readers will feel like they're riding a ship in rough seas. No one should want to make his or her readers feel sick. Keep your camera still and your subject in focus so that your readers can think about your subject rather than how much you're moving the camera.

That requires you to think ahead and anticipate the movement you'll be filming. If whatever you are shooting is going to be moving, frame the shot so that the subject is on the far side of the frame, so that you can see the subject move into the frame without having to move the camera. If the subject keeps moving, you can follow the subject for a while, then let the subject continue moving out of the frame to complete the shot.

I grew up in Indianapolis, so my favorite example of this type of shot is race cars at the Indy 500. The camera stays still as it picks up a car entering a turn, then moves to stay with the car through the middle of the turn. The camera eventually stops moving and lets the car go out of the frame as the car exits the turn. This way, the viewer can see the car through the entire turn, but with minimal camera movement.

It takes some experience to set your focus correctly before the shot, so that your subject will remain in focus throughout. Don't zoom in during your shot, either, if you can avoid it. Not only does a changing focus disorient your viewer, but also your microphone will pick up the ugly clicking sound of the camera's zoom mechanism shifting on certain cameras. Yuck. Position your camera and set the focus so that you won't need to adjust or zoom mid-shot.

A tripod is essential for maintaining a smooth and stable shot with video. Some cameras have stabilization features, and you can do some image stabilization with video editing software. But nothing helps you get a smooth, professional look to your video more than mounting your camera on a tripod. You can get a decent enough tripod for under $100, so invest in one if you anticipate shooting a lot of video.

While multi-shot, movement-filled, slickly-edited video packages can help drive traffic, you don't need to shoot and edit multiple shots to create a popular video online. Some of the most popular independent videos on YouTube are simple video blogs, where a subject sits in front of his or her laptop's webcam and speaks.

If you're recording yourself, either with a video camera or your laptop's built-in webcam, position the camera at your eye level, or above. That might mean you need to place your laptop on top of a stack of books to get the correct level. Shooting from eye level or above not only makes you look more attractive, it helps make you appear more friendly to the audience. If you shoot from below your eye level, your audience will see you "looking down" at them, which nobody likes.

Even if you do nothing more than shoot a weekly video blog where you talk about your biggest stories on the website in the past week, you'll reach viewers who prefer watching video to getting their information through reading text — readers you would have missed by publishing only a traditional, text-driven website. Adding newsworthy video clips to your presentation will help expand your audience even more.

On ThemeParkInsider.com, our most popular video clips are roller coaster videos, especially ones where I ride with someone from the theme park and we talk about the coaster as we ride. Since almost all theme parks prohibit holding cameras while riding, we have to produce these videos with the parks' cooperation during designated media days for new rides. (The park usually mounts a special camera to the ride frame to record us while riding.) Recently, we've started filming on "regular" park operating days using high-definition video cameras mounted inside eyeglasses, in order to record while not violating park safety rules prohibiting handheld cameras on their rides. We don't get the benefit of an interview while riding, but it allows us to get POV [point of view] video from older rides which debuted before our site, or from rides where we missed the official media day.

On Violinist.com, we would love to be able to post original performance video from top soloists, but recording labels aren't willing to give up any control over their artists' performances. So we either embed videos from labels and artists themselves, or we do without. We have had some success with posting instructional videos aimed at beginners, as well as posting an occasional video interview.

Interactivity

Writing, speaking, photos and video all move information in one direction — from you, the publisher, to your readers and viewers. But the Internet enables information to flow in all directions, not just from publisher to reader, but from reader back to publisher, and from reader to reader. How you solicit, manage and respond to information that flows from your readers will determine your business's success every bit as much as the quality of the information you publish. So you need to think about how you will handle interactivity in your publication.

I like to think of interactivity as a ladder. You want to make each step up the ladder seems as easy and as natural as possible for your readers. Start with a simple step — one that requires just a single mouse click and that doesn't reveal a reader's identity to anyone else on the site. For example, polls and votes provide a good first step toward engaging your readers as content creators on your website. Just one click on the poll and a reader has changed the content on your site — adding one to a tally. It might not seem like much, but that simplicity makes it a powerful introduction to more active participation in your website community.

Here are the steps on my ladder of engagement for website publishing:

- **Poll responses** — I use a custom polling tool that I wrote, which prohibits multiple votes from a single user account or IP address. You can find free polling tools built into some CMSs and available to everyone from sites such as Poll Daddy <*http://polldaddy.com*>.

- **Comments** — Once readers have voted in a poll, the next step is to encourage them to leave a comment about their votes. We run "vote of the week" features on both ThemeParkInsider.com and Violinist.com, specifically to draw "lurkers" into more active participation on the site. The questions we ask are ones we think will provoke great "bar arguments" — questions without proven answers but on which everyone's got an opinion. We want to make it so tempting to jump in with a comment after you click to vote that you just can't resist. And once someone's started commenting on a vote of the week post, he or she becomes more likely to comment elsewhere on the site as well.

- **Discussion responses** — There's not much difference between commenting on a blog post and responding to discussion thread. But in discussion forums the focus lies more on the community than it does on blogs, where the focus remains more on the writer of the original post. So this represents another step toward a more prominent role on the site.

- **Discussion questions** — This is a huge step, because now a reader is *initiating* content on your site, instead of simply responding to content posted by others. Still, there's no long-lasting commitment to the site when you post a new discussion thread — it's just one post. And you don't even need to put yourself out there by taking a stand on something. You simply could be asking a question.

- **Blogs** — Once readers start blogging on your site, they becomes your content partners. They're initiating content, and they're doing so in a form that often leads to a continuing relationship where readers keep posting content to your site. If you allow readers to blog for your publication, you'll want to think about how you manage their posts. On Violinist.com, we allow any registered member to start a blog, after a short waiting period. But those new blog posts are literally marginalized, linked to only from the right-side navigation column on our blog page. Our editor (my wife, Laurie) decides which of those posts to promote to running in full on the site's front page. On ThemeParkInsider.com, readers can submit individual posts to our front-page "Blog Flume", and I decide which ones to accept. But readers' posts aren't collected into individual blogs, as they are on Violinist.com, and if I reject a post for the Blog Flume, it is just deleted — it won't show up anywhere on the site.

You will want to offer your readers multiple opportunities to go from being a passive reader to becoming an active participant on your site. Social media buttons can help engage your readers by recruiting them as publicists for the content they like most. In addition to submitting discussion threads and blog posts, you might use plug-ins and other software tools to allow your readers to submit photos, video and audio tracks to your website, too. However you build your ladder of engagement, make sure that it has plenty of easy steps on it that will help your readers feel welcomed to step up.

I'd strongly consider leaving at least the first step on your ladder outside your registration system — so people can begin interacting with your site before having to make a commitment to register. Using a third-party system to manage comments, such as Facebook or Disqus <*http://disqus.com*> also can help lower the barrier to that step for the many readers who already have accounts on those systems. If you really want to move people up into blogging and active discussion participation, I wouldn't sacrifice your comments to a third-party app, but if that's going to be the top tier of interactivity on your site (at least at launch), it can be very nice to avoid having to install and manage your own registration system. Go ahead and think about Facebook or Disqus comments, then.

Whatever you choose, don't let anyone convince you that you can't manage interactivity on your website. That belief persists among some in the newspaper industry, thanks to a 1995 court ruling in a case called *Stratton Oakmont v. Prodigy*. In that case, the court held an online service liable for comments made by a user on the service's online forums because the service had hired community managers to monitor the forums. The United States Congress effectively nullified that ruling the next year, when it passed the Communications Decency Act of 1996, which created a "good Samaritan" exception that excused publishers from liability for comments made by users on their websites.

Stratton Oakmont profoundly influenced newspaper managers, who continued to insist to their employees for years after the CDA became law that they couldn't get involved in their websites' comments sections, lest the paper have to take responsibility for everything in those forums. And today, newspaper website comments sections rival YouTube's comment communities as the wretched refuse of the Internet — teeming shores providing homes to all strains of trolls and the perpetually angry.

You do *not* want your website to look like that.

Show some leadership instead. Nearly two decades of participating in online communities has taught me that a discussion board will adopt the tone and temperament of the individuals who post most often to the board. If you don't set an example for your readers, someone else will.

Approach leadership with a sense of humility, above all. This isn't about you or even your business. This online get-together exists to serve the needs of its community. It's about your readers. If you attract and retain them, the money can follow and your business will grow. Without readers, you have nothing.

And, as we've mentioned before (remember Dan Gillmor's quote from the previous chapter?), your readers — collectively — know more than you do, about pretty much anything. Get a conversation flowing by asking them about their experiences. Use those interviewing skills.

You'll start the best conversations by asking readers about their experiences rather than their opinions. Asking people about what they've done keeps the conversation grounded in reality, instead of spinning off into rumor and hearsay. Ask people about their opinions, and they're most likely to repeat stuff they've heard or read elsewhere. Whether that's true or not doesn't matter. People will repeat it if they think it sounds good. If you want truly original content on your site, ask readers about their personal, individual experiences, instead.

Participate in your conversations. Too many online writers throw open a discussion, then disappear. Simply showing up in your discussions or comment sections, with a follow-up question, or a even just a "thank you" now and then, sends your readers a powerful reminder than you're watching what they say. Readers love that. They want affirmation from "the people in charge," even if that's nothing more than a moment of time and attention. And readers want to know that someone is looking out for the community, too. Be that person, and you'll win the respect and loyalty of many readers.

Author Malcolm Gladwell had a best seller with his book *The Tipping Point*. You want your community to reach a "tipping point" where readers see others contributing smart, thoughtful comments, discussion threads and blog posts. Seeing that positive activity encourages the same. You want to avoid a tipping point where insults and misinformation rule on your site, attracting more insults as well as thoughtless comments copied from elsewhere on the Web.

Encourage your friends to join in your online conversations when your site debuts, so other readers see people talking on the site. No one wants to be the first one at a party. Your friends and action team can help push the conversation toward that positive tipping point, too. I also encourage new publishers to make posting on their sites as easy as possible for those first, new readers. On ThemeParkInsider.com, we continue to accept anonymous comments from our readers. Those comments don't appear immediately — I have to check and approve them first. But readers with something to say don't have to endure a registration process in order to submit a comment.

Your content management system might give you several options for handling registrations, comments and other forms of user input to your site. Since it is part of Google, Blogger users Google Accounts, which means that any of the millions of people who are logged into Google can be "logged in" to your site to leave a comment without going through another registration or log-in process. No matter which CMS you choose, you can opt to manage your website's comments through another service, such as Disqus or Facebook instead of through the CMS itself. Visit <*https://developers.facebook.com/docs/reference/plugins/comments*> to learn more about Facebook's commenting tool for websites. These comments also show up in the readers' Facebook timelines, helping spread word about your site to those readers' Facebook friends.

Ultimately, though, controlling your own registration process allows you to collect valuable information about your readers, as well as to create multiple levels of access (and control) that can give trusted readers more authority in your website community. While I encourage new publishers to make it as easy as possible for early readers to submit comments — to build to that tipping point of activity on the website — readers will be willing to register for your website specifically once they see enough benefit from becoming an "official" member of the community. On Violinist.com, we run contests to give away autographed CDs, classical music downloads, tickets to orchestra contests, website T-shirts and music bags, among other prizes. But we only allow people who have registered with the website to enter — so that's one way we create a benefit for registration.

On both of our websites, we ask our readers to register using their real names, as we believe that policy encourages people to behave online. But we have created an exception for theme park employees posting to ThemeParkInsider.com. We ask them to register under an assumed name, since no parks allow their employees to post online about the park with authorization from the park's publicity department (which, let's face it, our ~~snitches~~ readers aren't getting). As I mentioned, we also allow anonymous comments on ThemeParkInsider.com, but those have to be approved by an editor before they appear. If a comment's abusive or spammy, we simply delete it before anyone else has the opportunity to read it.

Of course, I've seen "real name only" communities online that felt like verbal cesspools compared with other communities that allowed anonymous and pseudonymous posts. Ultimately, a site's leadership determines the tone of the community. No matter which policies you choose about registration, back them up with strong leadership — from you and your action team.

At some point, you'll have to step back and let your community police itself. As any parent knows, eventually, your children have to find their own way in the world. You can't keep doing everything for them, forever. Nor should you. Be aggressive in the early days after you launch in confronting bullies, spammers and others who would compromise your board. But at some point — and only you will know when — you should pause and wait a while before taking on a rogue poster. Wait to see how your community of readers responds. If the response doubles down on the nastiness, jump in. You'll know that your community's still in kindergarten and needs to be watched.

But if the next post confronts the bully, and the bully backs down or goes away, go out and celebrate that night. You'll know that you've reached an important milestone in the history of your publication — the point when your community has grown up enough that it can begin to police itself.

Your community's not fully grown at that point, of course. You and your action team will need to continue to use your influence to keep the community moving forward. But it sure is nice when your readers begin to see enough value in what you and your team have started that *they* want to work to protect it, too.

Your Public Persona

When I went to journalism school, I heard more than a few classmates and professors warn: "Don't do anything you wouldn't want to see printed on the front page of *The New York Times*." The idea was that journalists are watching, and if you do something wrong, you could be found out. Of course, even in the heyday of newspaper journalism, reporters couldn't be everywhere, and quite a bit of wrongdoing never showed up on any page of any newspaper.

Today, life's different. Search engines and social media make *anything* published online as easy to find as the stuff on the front page of today's NYT. So let's amend the advice: Do not post anything online that you wouldn't want the entire world — including all your audience and customers — to see.

What do you have up on the Web right now that you might not want the people you're asking to fund your website to see? Pictures on Facebook? Posts on Twitter? Discussion board rants? If anyone wants to find something online that embarrasses or humiliates you, if it's up anywhere, someone will find it.

Think of it this way: Your business now is getting people to pay attention to what you do. If you are successful, it means that people will now be paying attention to what you do. Are you ready to accept full responsibility for that?

Be as aggressive in projecting and protecting a good personal reputation online as you are with any other aspect of your business. Have you registered your domain name? I'm not talking about your publication's domain name. I'm talking about *yourfirstnameyourlastname.com*. If it is available, go get it right now. Don't worry about building a website for it yet. Just secure the domain before anyone else can get it. Once you become a public person, someone else will try to register it — and you might not like the result. Your name is your personal brand and you want to protect it online as aggressively as you will protect the brand of your publication. Register Twitter, Facebook, YouTube, Gmail and other social media accounts for your name, if you haven't done that already.

If you've established those accounts already, go back through them and look at what you've posted there. If you need to delete any potentially embarrassing content, do it now — don't wait. And resolve to be a better Internet citizen going forward.

I have a personal Twitter account and Facebook page, in addition to Twitter and Facebook accounts for ThemeParkInsider.com. I consider these completely different voices and maintain strict personal rules about what I'll post to each account. I like to talk about politics, sports, business and Internet culture on my @robertniles Twitter account. Those are my interests, and I love engaging with other Twitter users to discuss them. But I would never post anything remotely political on my @themepark Twitter account. That's the voice of ThemeParkInsider.com, and I keep it much more sharply focused.

If you'll be maintaining more than one Twitter account, be very careful about remembering which account you're logged into before you post. You don't want to end up like the American Red Cross' social media staffer who in February 2011 forgot which account she was logged into, and posted to the Red Cross Twitter account:

"Ryan found two more 4 bottle packs of Dogfish Head's Midas Touch beer.... when we drink we do it right #gettngslizzerd"

Whoops! To its credit, the Red Cross handled this incident spectacularly well, owning up to its staffer's mistake and showing a sense of humor about it. It Tweeted:

"We've deleted the rogue tweet but rest assured the Red Cross is sober and we've confiscated the keys."

The beer company referenced in the original Tweet helped turn the episode into a win by asking its followers to donate to the Red Cross, and Tweet about it when they did — using the hashtag #gettngslizzerd, of course.

Your private interaction with readers and customers also will influence your public persona. How many times have you seen tabloid stories citing unnamed waiters or house staff tattling about their work with celebrities? If your business becomes as popular as you hope it will be, its success will make you a celebrity of sorts within your community. If you treat a reader or customer rudely — no matter how badly they deserved it, in your view — expect word about that to get around.

Don't blow up at your readers. Ever. No matter how much one might provoke you. Not only is being nice the good and decent thing to do, it will help protect your public persona. Imagine the TMZ cameras on you at all times, and respond to both questions and provocations alike with grace. Respond promptly to emails (with 24 hours, at most), and try to be kind when you do.

My go-to answer — even if I have nothing to say — is "thank you for writing." If someone's taken the time to reach out to you, that's the very least you owe him or her in return. Try not to assume that an emotional email or phone call is hostile, as difficult as that might be. It could be that the person contacting you is just really passionate about an issue, and that's coming across as a confrontational tone. Your job, as publisher, is to be the grown-up and handle the situation with patience and maturity.

And do not forget that, sometimes, the mature response is to gracefully end the conversation. Thank someone for writing or calling, then end it. While you should try to diffuse and resolve situations, bail when you get to the point where you feel this is turning into abuse. You don't deserve that. Resist the urge to lash out, or take a parting shot — just get away.

Fortunately, in my experience, almost all of my contact with readers has been positive. On February 29, 2012, Disneyland and Walt Disney World's Magic Kingdom ran promotions where those theme parks would be open for 24 consecutive hours on Leap Day. With thousands of Disney theme park fans, I lined up to enter Disneyland when the park opened for its 24-hour run at 6 a.m. that morning. I'd decided that I would Tweet what I was doing throughout the day, so readers who couldn't get to the parks could visit vicariously, through me.

So a little after 7 a.m., I Tweeted that I was about to get on the Astro Orbitor ride — those little two-person rocket jets that spin in a circle at the front of the park's Tomorrowland. Just 15 seconds later, a person who also was waiting to board stepped over to me and asked, "Are you Robert Niles?" He'd been following my Tweets, and realized that I must be in the same queue as he was. He looked around and found the guy who looked like my picture from the site, and decided to say hello. I met several other ThemeParkInsider.com readers in the park that day, using social media to find each other.

Confession time: I am one of the shyest, most socially anxious and pathetically insecure people you will ever meet, but I find a way to put that aside whenever I meet a reader. How? I think about how having readers makes my business possible. Without the loyal attention and support of my publication's readers, I wouldn't be able to have the publishing job I love so much. That gratitude allows me to get over my anxiety and shyness, and to smile, be happy and thankful with every reader I meet. And once I'm past my initial fear, I can see the really cool person in front of me, someone with whom I usually have much more than a website community in common.

Your website's brand starts with you — with your personal brand. You will become the initial face of your website, and the way you approach, treat and respond to people will define the way people feel about your publication. And it will inspire your website's action team as it interacts with new and potential site supporters as well. The personal touch matters, even for an online publication. A hundred articles on a website won't make the impression upon a reader that saying hello and talking with him in a Disneyland queue can.

EXERCISE

Register *yourfirstnameyourlastname* as a .com Internet domain, and as an account name on Facebook, Twitter and other social networks, if you have not yet done that and they're still available.

Once you have a Twitter account — start using it. Read my former co-worker Steve Buttry's excellent advice on using Twitter for inspiration: <http://stevebuttry.wordpress.com/2012/08/06/advice-and-examples-on-how-and-what-journalists-should-tweet>. Then resolve to Tweet at least 10 times a day for the next 10 days just to get into the habit. Use this as an excuse to further sharpen your observational skills, as you look around for interesting scenes and details in your community to Tweet. Tell friends about your Twitter account, use hashtags, follow others who Tweet about things you find interesting, and when someone responds to your Tweets, respond back to continue the conversation.

9 EVALUATE YOUR WORK THROUGH ANALYTICS

You've turned in your work. Now it's time to get your grade.

As a publisher, you might think that you get to decide how to judge the success or failure of your publication. Ultimately, you don't. Your customers will determine your publication's success. But how will tell what your customers have decided? How will you know your grade?

Internet publishing generates a vast amount of data that details how readers consume your website — hard data that businesses simply can't get in print or broadcasting. If you've ever worked as an employee in online publishing, your bosses might have used some of these analytics in evaluating your performance in your job: unique visitors, pageviews, time spent on site, etc. In offline media, publishers traditionally have used random-sample surveys of their audience or conducted focus groups to approximate this data. But Web servers collect *real* usage data that can be analyzed in many different ways to generate many different reports.

As a publisher, however, only one metric really matters in

judging the success or failure of your business: ***How much money did you make?*** If you're not making money, you're not a business — you're a hobby, and a potentially expensive one at that. If you're not making money, you need to find ways to cut expenses or raise revenues — or both — in order to get your business profitable. Otherwise, you'll need to either try a different business, or resign yourself to returning to work as an employee instead of pursuing your dreams as an entrepreneur.

But don't give up right away. Take a hard look at some of that traffic and usage data. They provide the clues that can lead you down a path toward making more money. You simply need to learn how to find and read those clues. In this chapter, I'll define many of the analytics you'll encounter as an online publisher, so you'll know the difference between terms such as "hits" and "pageviews." I'll also go through some of the strategies you can use to improve readership and profitability.

Let me warn you about a couple traps data can set for you, however.

First, the massive amount of data you can access as an online publisher can overwhelm you. It's "***paralysis by analysis***" and that can cripple businesses when they need to make swift changes to better serve their markets.

To be fair, though, paralysis by analysis does keep millions of people employed as business consultants, analysts and other assorted middle managers. All those number-crunchers can be your best friends — when they're working for your competition, inflating their costs by spending time and money generating reports, instead of making smart decisions that move those competitors forward.

Don't make those same mistakes in your business. Learn how to understand analytics and use them wisely.

Second, beware something called "***confirmation bias***." That's the tendency people have to cherry-pick the data that affirms their beliefs, while ignoring the information that contradicts them.

With all the data available to you as a publisher, it's not that hard to find specific analytics that look good — no matter how badly your site might be foundering. Don't fall in love with data that shows you've got hundreds of comments pouring into your discussion board each day... while ignoring visitor analytics that try to show you those comments are coming from the same dozen or so readers. And don't get too excited by visitor data that shows you're reaching thousands of daily readers... if a deeper look at that data shows that more than 90 percent of those readers are first-time visitors who'll never return. Look for the complete picture.

How do we get this analytics data you're supposed to be watching? You've got some options.

Analytics data comes from one of two places. Your Web server will maintain something called a "log file." A "log file" records the name of every file on the server that it delivers to readers on the Internet, the time it sent the file and where the server sent it. When the server records that data, it will include a bunch of information it gets from the computer that's requesting the file, including its reader's IP address and the name and version number of the operating system and browser of the reader's computer, tablet or cell phone. You can run an analytics program on this log file, which will parse those hard-to-read records and create a wide range of easy-to-read reports based on their data.

The other source for analytics data is from what's called "page tagging." Think of this as outsourcing your analytics. Instead of looking at data from your Web server's own log files, tag-based systems look at data that's collected by a third party that's tracking your website. You put a few lines of HTML code from that third party into your website's page templates, and whenever a reader loads your page, the third party collects the log file data about that request — including the page requested and all the available location, operating system and browser data about the reader making the request.

Why would you bring a third party into this process? Why not just use your own Web server's log files? Here's the issue: Many of the "readers" requesting pages on your website aren't really people at all. A huge percentage of traffic on the Internet is from what we call automated agents — computer programs sent out to track and index content online. Google's "Googlebot" is the most famous of these "robots" (or "bots"), but millions of others scour the Internet, every second of every minute of every hour of every day. Some are looking for published email addresses to harvest for spam email lists. Others are looking for articles or discussion posts that mention a particular product or company. Many are looking for weaknesses in content management systems, so that they can post spam messages and viruses to poorly defended websites.

In my experience, up to 90 percent of the overall traffic on some sites I've managed has come from automated agents. When you look at an analytics program, you want to see data from real people, not from bots. Now, that bot data is important to have, especially if your site becomes the target of an attack. But for day-to-day analysis, and especially for numbers you will show to potential customers, you want to see the data from actual human readers.

Page-tagging services, such as Google Analytics <http://analytics.google.com>, filter most of the automated traffic from your analytics reports, giving you a clearer picture of your human readership. Many Web hosting services provide analytics programs to look at your server's log files, but you might have to create and maintain your own filters of automated agents to exclude from your reports. Why spend hours every week keeping those filters up to date when Google will do that work for you, for free? (We use Google Analytics on our websites.)

Page-tagging services are far from perfect. Most won't count readers who have javascript disabled in their browsers, so you'll have to accept that as a trade-off for their ease of use if you choose them. But I consider Google Analytics a usable analytics solution. Other page-tracking services, such as Quantcast

<http://www.quantcast.com> and Compete <http://www.compete.com>, can be useful in comparing your website's traffic data to other sites that use those same services. I wouldn't bother looking at the traffic data these services estimate for other websites that don't use their tracking codes. Traffic estimates based on random sample surveys of Internet users are highly inaccurate for anything other than wildly popular websites. (In case you are wondering, Google Analytics doesn't allow you to see how your site ranks versus others. That's the market need that Compete and Quantcast are trying to fill.)

Any analytics service you use will require that you understand certain terms and concepts. Let's define some:

Website analytics vocabulary list

Dimension: A dimension is any individual category in an analytics report — such as the number of visitors in a given time period, the type of browsers used by visitors, the location of visitors, etc.

Metrics: A metric is any dimension that can be expressed with a number. Examples include number of page views, time spent on the site, visitors per day/week/month, etc.

Hits: A hit is any request for any file on your server, which generates a line in your server's log file. So if a reader visits your home page, that will generate one hit for the home page file request, as well as an additional hit for every image file, style sheet, or other file on your server that's embedded on that page. On a large, complicated webpage, a single viewing of a page by a single reader can generate dozens of "hits." That's why "hits" is the single most useless metric online. No one with any serious Web publishing experience uses the term. If you see the word "hits" in a news article about Internet traffic, you now know that the reporter who wrote the piece knows little or nothing about the Internet. Let us never speak of hits again.

Bandwidth: The total number of bytes (or megabytes, gigabytes or terabytes) of all the files served by your Web server over a specific period of time. Many Web hosting services charge you if you go over a certain bandwidth allocation in a billing period, so pay attention to this metric. Page-tagging services such as Google Analytics will *not* track this data, so you'll have to watch it via your Web host's account maintenance page. Many hosts will email you a warning if you are approaching your limit, too.

Pageviews: This is the number of webpage files viewed on your server. This metric is most useful as the basis for determining how much ad inventory you'll have available to sell. The number of ads you display per page, times the number of pageviews you serve in a month, is the number of ads you have available to sell that month.

Visits: Every time a reader comes to your website and starts reading pages, that's a visit. You might think that's a useful description of the size of your audience, but the better metric is...

Unique visitors: Some readers come to your website more than once a day/week/month/whenever. "Unique visitors" ignores subsequent visits from the same visitors to give you the total number of actual, distinct individuals who've visited your site over a given period. This is the size of your audience — the total number of unique people you reach in a selected period of time.

Bounce rate: This is the percentage of visits to your site where the visitor viewed only one page. (Then they "bounced" off to some other website.)

Exit rate: This rate applies to individual pages. It is the percentage of visitors for whom this particular page was the last one they viewed before leaving the site.

Time spent: The "time spent" on a particular page is the time between the request for that page, and the next request for another page on your site by the same visitor. The server will not record the time spent on the last page on your site a visitor sees, because there will be no subsequent request from that visitor in the log files. The "time spent on site" is the time between the first request by a visitor and the last request on that visit. (It will necessarily undercount the actual time spent on the site, because the server won't know how long the visitor spent on his or her final page.) After 30 minutes between requests from a single visitor, Google Analytics counts the second request as the start of a new visit.

Now let's talk about some terms often used in describing online advertising:

Impressions: This is the number of ads shown over a period of time.

Click-throughs: This is the number of times that visitors clicked a particular ad. (They "click through" to the ad's destination. The "click-through URL" is the webpage where the reader is directed when he or she clicks the ad.)

CTR: Click-through rate — the number of click-throughs divided by the number of impressions for a particular ad. You can track clicks and CTR by individual ad, campaign, ad position or page. The overall CTR data for individual ad positions on a page is helpful because it tells you where on the page readers are most likely to click on ads. The CTR for particular categories of pages on your site can tell you in which sections of your site readers are most likely to click. That's helpful as you try to optimize your site's design to make your ads more attractive to potential customers.

As we've written before, you can price your ads in one of three ways:

CPM: Cost per *mille* — The cost (in dollars or whatever currency) you charge an advertiser for 1,000 ad impressions delivered in a specific ad position on your site. (*Mille* is French for "thousand." "M" also is the Roman numeral for one thousand.) You get paid when readers see ads, no matter how those readers respond (or don't).

CPC: Cost per click — The cost you charge an advertiser each time a reader clicks an ad. In a CPC system, you get paid only when readers click the ads they see on your site.

CPA: Cost per action — The cost you charge an advertiser when a reader takes a specific action after clicking an ad or a link displayed on your website. This is essentially a commission system, where you get paid for each sale or registration an advertiser gets from the readers you send its way. Amazon's Associates Program <*http://associates.amazon.com*> is one of the Web's most widely-used CPA advertising system.

We use Google's DoubleClick for Publishers <*http://www.google.com/dfp*> system to serve and track ads on our websites. Like Google Analytics, it's free to publishers and easy to use. The DFP system generates custom reports tracking impression delivery, clicks and CTR, while allowing you to schedule ad campaigns for specified numbers of impressions at whatever CPM or CPC you can sell them. You can target campaigns by geographic location, time of day, ad position on your pages or section of your website — depending upon how you set up your rate card. You also can let Google sell your unsold ad inventory through its AdSense network.

But where should you place those ads on your pages? And how do you do that?

The Internet Advertising Bureau has established a handful of standard ad sizes for websites, so that advertisers aren't stuck making different banner ad files to fit in different sized ad positions on thousands of different websites. If you want to attract ad revenue from major advertisers (or ad revenue from networks such as Google's AdSense), the banner ads on your website will need to be these sizes.

The three most popular IAB ad sizes are:

- A 160-pixels wide by 600-pixels tall "Wide Skyscraper" ad

- A 728-pixels wide by 90-pixels tall "Leaderboard" ad
- A 300-pixels wide by 250-pixels tall "Medium Rectangle" ad

We use all three on ThemeParkInsider.com and Violinist.com. I'd suggest that you experiment with all three ad formats, placing them in positions within your page design where you think they'll attract the attention of interested readers. Google has conducted lab research in which they tracked the eyes of readers who were shown several website designs. From that, Google's created "heat maps" that show where readers were most likely to look on certain page designs. You can see some of the results of Google's research at <*http://support.google.com/adsense/bin/answer.py?hl=en&answer=1354747*> (Or search on Google for "eyetrack heat map adsense".)

Other researchers have conducted similar eye-tracking studies, and they often find similar results: Readers tend to see webpages in an "F"-shaped pattern. Imagine a large letter F superimposed over the design of a webpage. Readers' eyes are most likely to focus on content underneath that letter "F" — the top horizontal row along the upper edge of the page, the content along the left side, and another horizontal row of content a little farther down the page. If you place your ads in one of these areas, you'll maximize the attention they get, as well as the number of readers who click on those ads.

Over the years, I've used a process called **A/B testing** to find the best positions for ads on our websites. In A/B testing, you put up two versions of something — an "A" sample and a "B" sample. Then you see how each sample performs. The key is to make sure that you change only *one* thing between the two samples, such as the position of an ad on the page. If you change more than one variable on the page, you won't be able to know for certain which of those variables was responsible for any difference in performance between the A and the B samples.

Ideally, you could instruct your content management system

to randomly select one of two templates to display when a reader visits a page, one with the A sample and the other with the B sample. If your CMS can't do that, or you haven't been able to figure out how to make that happen, don't sweat. You can just try one sample for a period of time, such as a day, then switch to the other sample. It won't be a clean A/B test, due to the time difference, but for a small-scale start-up, it should be good enough to show you if there's any major difference in performance between your A and B options.

How will you determine which option performed better? Here's where you use your metrics. Compare the CPM earnings for each option in an ad-placement A/B test, to see which one earned you more money. If you're testing site design elements, see if one option led to more pageviews per visitor or more time spent on site. You can use A/B testing to evaluate major changes, such as different WordPress themes (if you're using that particular CMS) as well as simpler modifications, such as whether a different typeface leads to people reading your site longer or where to place social media buttons to elicit the most number of "Likes" or "Tweets" for individual posts.

Don't let "paralysis by analysis" slow you when you're launching your site. Go with a design that you believe best expresses the tone and functionality you wish to deliver — a design that you think will connect well with your intended audience. But don't forget that you'll be collecting plenty of analytics — information from your audience that you can use to tweak (or overhaul) your design as you work to increase your audience and income over time.

In my testing of ad positions on our websites, I've found that placing a Wide Skyscraper along the left side of the page and a Medium Rectangle in the middle of the page, in between the first and second post on that page, generates the most revenue. On ThemeParkInsider.com, where I have a relatively wide right navigation column, I also place another Medium Rectangle ad position at the top of that column. On Violinist.com, I place a Leaderboard ad near the bottom of the page, instead. (Google allows you up to three AdSense banner ads per page — so you can't place any more positions on the page if you'll be selling them through the AdSense network.)

Once you've selected where to place ads on your page, how will you decide what you should charge for them? Ultimately, your customers will make this decision for you. The right price is the highest one that sells out your available inventory. If you're left with a lot of unsold ads, you're either not working hard enough to sell or you're charging too much. If you sell out your inventory easily, you might be leaving money on the table by charging too little for those ads.

But you've got to start someplace before you can find the "right" price for your ads. Here's what I did: I just let Google sell the ads on my sites for a while, before I tried to sell my own ads. I spent my time focusing on content and building my audience. I did some A/B testing to find the best positions and sizes for ads on the site, then noted how much CPM I was making from each ad position.

When businesses started coming to me to buy ads on the site, I just doubled the CPM I was getting from Google and used that as my initial asking price. Within a year or so, I was selling most of the inventory on the site each month, so I figure that I was charging a fair price. But I was spending way to much time with each advertiser, explaining the meaning of CPM and other metrics I was using.

That's when I decided that I should create a simpler rate card — one that charged advertisers a fixed amount for a specific number of ad impressions. Each of the dollar amounts I decided to charge worked out to the same CPM, but advertisers found it much easier to wrap their heads around a $200 or a $500 ad package than trying to do the math to figure out what they'd be getting from a "$5 CPM" buy. Remember, "most local advertisers don't know how to spell 'CPM'."

So don't force that on them. Do the CPM math yourself and offer easy-to-understand price points to your potential customers. I consider "time spent explaining tech stuff to advertisers" to be another important metric for my business. And that's a metric I like to keep as close to zero as possible. I much prefer to spend my time with customers listening to their problems and offering my potential solutions to them. Customers just want you to take their pain away. The easier you make that for them, the more customers you'll win and the more you'll retain.

You can use analytics to adjust your editorial coverage to connect better with your audience as well. But don't look only for the most popular articles on your website and try to duplicate them. I'll bet that your audience doesn't want to keep reading the same types of pieces over and over again (remember the omelette from last chapter?), and I'll also bet that you don't want to keep reporting and writing the same thing over and over again, either. Chasing success is a great way to burn yourself out.

The better way to use analytics to help shape your coverage is to look at the *other* end of the pageview report. Note which articles get *little or no* traffic. Find the least popular types of articles on your site... and stop producing so many of them. Spend your time on other topics or types of articles instead and see if they do better.

If you think these poorly-read articles cover important topics, listen to the data anyway, and admit that your pieces aren't connecting with the readers you want to reach. Let your readership metrics push you at least to try different ways of explaining or presenting this information, to connect better with your audience.

And if you didn't think much of those little-read articles anyway, well, take some comfort in that your readers agreed with you. Ditch 'em, and move on to something else. On ThemeParkInsider.com, I've paid close attention over the years to the data we've collected on how many people have read articles about or submitted reader reviews for specific theme parks around the world. Low numbers tell me that readers just don't care that much about particular parks. Because I want to serve my readers, I now spend less time covering those parks, leaving me more time to explore stories from other parks.

Again, don't just turn around and try to duplicate your successful stories. Use this as an excuse to explore new territory. I've received some great response over the years covering Holiday World, a small, family-run theme park in the tiny town of Santa Claus, Indiana — located about an hour west of Louisville. The park doesn't show up among the Top 20 most-visited theme parks in the United States, so you might expect that there wouldn't be much public interest in the park. But Holiday World does several things that merit attention. It doesn't charge for parking, and it offers free, unlimited soft drinks and sunscreen to its visitors. The park also has built three of the best wooden-track roller coasters in the world. It's got one of the world's better water parks, too, which is included in the theme park admission. All this makes the park a great value — the type of hidden gem that theme park fans love to discover.

I wouldn't have had the time to explore Holiday World if I'd still been paying so much attention to some of the more-visited, but less-loved, theme parks I had been covering. I needed to drop the coverage my readers didn't want in order to give me the time (and free up my travel budget) to cover what they did want.

I love hearing from my readers, through email, social media or in person. But only my analytics reports give me a complete picture of what my *entire* audience thinks about my publication. Analytics tell me who my audience is, and how they've reacted to what I've done. They're the letter grade for my work, and if I really care about serving my audience, I need to pay attention to what the audience is trying to tell me, through my readership analytics.

EXERCISE

Set up a Google Analytics account <*http://www.google.com/analytics*> and a DoubleClick for Publishers <*http://www.google.com/dfp*> account. Click the "Learn more" links on each of those pages to get more familiar with these services.

The easiest way to create these accounts is to create and log into a Google Account, then use that to set up both these other accounts. If you already have a Google Account, you might think about creating another one, specifically for your business identity, especially if your current Google Account is associated with a personal YouTube or Gmail account that you won't want associated with your business. (Remember what I wrote earlier about conducting yourself as a public person?) One easy way to keep your Google Accounts separate is to use different browsers for each.

10 GROW YOUR BUSINESS BY REPEATING THE PROCESS

Let's review. Over the past six chapters, I've introduced six steps of a process for launching your online publishing business, based on the classic principles of community organizing. You will start by assessing the community you want to serve, learning its needs. Then you will develop relationships and find helpful resources to build an action team to assist you on this project. After that, you'll develop an action plan, creating a checklist of things to do to make your business real. Then it's time to mobilize — gathering information for your publication and engaging your action team through personal contact and social media. The next-to-last step will be to launch — to publish your site using a variety of presentation formats, including writing, photography, video and discussion. Then you will wrap it up by evaluating the success of your work through the use of website analytics reports.

But you won't be finished after that last step in the process. Every time you complete the cycle, you'll follow up by returning to the first step, and doing this all over again.

This seven-step cycle can guide you through every aspect of

running a publishing business. For every post you publish on your site, you should follow these seven steps: (1) Take a look around. (2) Find sources. (3) Figure out what information you need from your sources. (4) Collect it. (5) Write it up or otherwise present it. (6) Check the analytics to see how the post did. (7) Repeat with another post.

You'll do the same for each ad you sell: (1) Look for businesses that need to reach your audience. (2) Identify the decision-makers at those businesses. (3) Plan your approach. (4) Meet and ask for the sale. (5) Collect the money and put up the ad. (6) Measure the ad's performance and report back to the customer. (7) Repeat with another potential customer.

The community organizing model works when you're expanding your business into new projects, as well as for daily maintenance of the site. In this chapter, I'll tell you about three major projects we've taken on over the years at ThemeParkInsider.com and Violinist.com. I hope that they will inspire you to think of unconventional ways to expand your business, using the community organizing model.

Accident Watch

Like many journalists who'd moved into online publishing in the 1990s, I'd first started using computers in my journalism career to help analyze large datasets for reporting projects. I'd played around with a Federal Aviation Administration database that allowed users to look up the safety record of any registered aircraft in the United States by entering the unique "N" number displayed on its tail. And I knew that many state highway patrol departments collected databases of injury accidents on state highways, too.

These projects gave me the idea to include links in our database of rides at Disney and Universal theme parks to reported injury accidents at those rides. In 1998, a Disneyland visitor was killed when a park employee improperly attempted to moor the sailing ship *Columbia* in the park's Frontierland section. The park employee threw a mooring rope around a cleat on the ship before it has slowed to the appropriate speed. The rope tore the cleat from the moving boat, which flew into a waiting crowd, striking and killing the visitor. Also that year, a 5-year-old boy's foot was crushed when he was trying to get off the park's Big Thunder Mountain Railroad roller coaster. These incidents prompted my readers to start talking about theme park safety, and I wanted to provide them with some hard data about injury incidents on various rides. (That was step one — assessing the community and finding the need — in this case, for more information about theme park injury accidents.)

At that point, I looked for the federal database tracking theme park accidents, and I discovered that there wasn't one. Federal law didn't authorize any agency to collect this information. Nor were there any state databases tracking injury accidents. California would soon begin recording accidents, but state officials would define "injury accidents" only as ones that required overnight hospitalization or the missing of school or work. A child who broke his arm on a ride during summer vacation — and didn't stay overnight in the hospital or miss a day of school as a result — wouldn't be counted as an injury accident victim under this definition.

If I was going to provide this information to my readers, I was going to have to find another source for the data. Existing news reports weren't sufficient. Those two Disneyland accidents had made the local papers, but I knew from personal experience working at the Walt Disney World Resort that many other injury accidents did not. For example, one evening while I was working in the Magic Kingdom, a visitor had suffered a major eye injury when his boat stuck at the bottom of the drop on Pirates of the Caribbean and another boat crashed on top of his boat.

No local media outlet reported that incident, but every employee I knew in the park heard about it. From my experience publishing ThemeParkInsider.com, I knew that hundreds of park employees were reading the site, and that on any given day, several dozen site readers were visiting the parks we covered. I figured that if something big enough to hurt someone happened in the parks, some of our readers would hear about it. So I decided to turn to our readers as the sources for our accident database.

My readers would become my action team for this project. I recruited other help, as well, including the mother of the boy who'd been hurt on Thunder Mountain at Disneyland. She was leading a lobbying effort to get California to do a better job of recording accidents in theme parks.

I had an eager action team in place, but I couldn't ask them to collect information until I knew exactly what information I wanted them to collect. For step three, I needed a specific action plan — a detailed structure for the data I wanted to collect and display. I created a scheme for a new table in my site's database to house the injury data, and I designed a flowchart for how I'd handle that information. I decided that I'd treat any single report of an injury accident as unverified, until I had a second source to confirm the report. I'd publish the unverified reports, but label them as such, so that other readers could either confirm or dispute the report. For step four, I mobilized by creating the table in the database and building the Web forms that would allow readers to input, confirm and dispute accident reports.

We implemented Accident Watch in early 2001, launching the feature with a discussion board post that explained the feature and invited all ThemeParkInsider.com readers to participate. Within a few weeks, I, my action team, and other readers of the site had input and verified dozens of injury accidents at various parks from the past several years. We also had started new discussions sharing safety tips, in an effort to better educate park visitors on how to avoid becoming an accident victim.

How to assess the project? The project helped increase traffic to the website, as the injury accident pages drew several hundred pageviews per day. But we were looking for the project to do more than that. It's impossible to measure a negative — we could never know for certain if our work had helped prevent an injury or a death in a theme park, as we'd hoped it would. But the project did help draw more public attention to the issue of safety in theme parks. As a result of the project, I was invited to speak on several major broadcast news programs, including the CBS Evening News.

And in October 2001, the Columbia Graduate School of Journalism and the Online News Association honored ThemeParkInsider.com with an Online Journalism Award in Service Journalism for Accident Watch. It was the first instance of a major journalism award going to an online news project crowdsourced by reader-submitted reports. Today, state governments in both California and Florida have strengthened their reporting of accidents in theme parks, and local papers in Orlando and Southern California routinely file stories based on quarterly injury accident reports from theme parks.

Violinist.com Business Directory

We've been grateful to enjoy the support of many sponsors on Violinist.com. Over the years, we've attracted ads from top music schools, major instrument retailers, luthiers (violin makers) and people selling all sorts of violin accessories. But we've also discovered that while we are selling to a wide variety of customers, the actual ad placements we've been selling them don't vary much at all.

Some of our sponsors sell violins that cost many thousands of dollars. They're happy to spend quite a bit of money for every click on their ads from Violinist.com readers, because the profit for just one sale to a reader would be worth hundreds, perhaps even thousands, of dollars. Other sponsors sell things such as shoulder rests, sheet music and practicing apps — items that sell for just a few dollars, orders of magnitude less than the fine violins promoted in other ads on the site. As a result, these sponsors can't afford to spend more than a few cents per lead, as anything more than that would wipe out the meager profit they make on each sale.

By pricing our banner ads at the same CPM across the site, we'd inadvertently made it impossible for both types of advertisers to succeed on our website. If we tried to maximize our income — as any sane business would — by charging the highest CPM we could get, the big-budget instrument retailers would crowd out the other businesses that sell to lower price points. They just couldn't afford to buy ads at those rates and still make money. If we cut our ad prices to try to accommodate those lower-priced retailers, the big retailers would have even more incentive to buy out our discounted inventory, and we'd be leaving money on the table.

Retailers selling at lower price points, with tighter profit margins, simply need a different ad product than retailers selling the luxury cars of the violin world. So there was the market need. How could we fulfill it?

We already had built relationships with several advertisers, including some that had left because they couldn't get the sales volume they needed with the relatively low number of ad impressions they could afford to buy from us. But we needed to extend our reach. My wife long had been a member of a national association of string music teachers, since she's been teaching private violin students for more than a decade. She told me that the group had an "industry council" of violin businesses that sponsored the teachers' association. We joined the council, as Violinist.com, and sent my wife to the association's annual convention to make contacts with many of the businesses that exhibited there.

Don't overlook the importance of showing other businesses in your community that you support that community, too. Sure, you're serving the community through meeting specific needs. But it's important for you to act as a good citizen in the local business community as well. Joining a business council supporting string music teachers helped us to show that Violinist.com was a good business citizen. Donating to local public schools, sponsoring youth sports teams or joining a local retailers' association can help you demonstrate your citizenship, while connecting you with other businesses that support the same causes.

This provides another way for you to build relationships and to expand your action team. At this stage, we weren't selling anyone a new ad product — we were trying to figure out what that ad product would be. So we tried to connect with additional businesses by asking them about their experiences with online advertising, and then we considered what we heard back from them as we thought about our next step.

Remembering the line that "most people can't spell CPM," we soon decided that we needed a simpler product — one that we could sell for a low, flat price and that didn't involve ad rotations or any other complicated technical stuff that would make it hard for smaller sponsors to see what they were buying.

That led us to decide on a business directory. But what would it look like? And how would we direct our readers to it? Time for an action plan.

I looked at *a lot* of directory pages online, trying to find graphical and content elements I thought would appeal to both our readers and our advertisers. Since I was trying to keep costs low on these listings, I decided that it just didn't make sense to build a new section of our content management system to handle the number of listings I thought we could sell. Instead, we'd create a simple, old-school, flat-file HTML page. With a limited number of participants, on annual contracts, we wouldn't be changing the content of that page much, anyway.

(Tech note: I used the goo.gl link shortener <*http://goo.gl*> in order to track the number of clicks to each sponsor's website from the directory, and the *rel=nofollow* attribute in the links' anchor tags, per Google's guidelines for paid advertising links.

Please take a look at <http://support.google.com/webmasters/bin/answer.py?answer=96569> for more information on when you should use a nofollow attribute when building Web links.)

That process answered the question about what the directory would look like. Now, how to drive readers? We decided to change our top navigation bar to reduce the number of pages displayed there, even while saving one spot on the nav bar for our new directory page. We also decided to change the background color for the link to the directory page, to help it stand out. (The fact that this would be the only commercial option in the bar, among a bunch of editorial features, also helped us to decided that it needed to look different, graphically.)

In addition, I decided to create a simple list of text links to all of our sponsors' websites, and to include that in the right-side navigation on all other Violinist.com pages. This increased the value of sponsorship to all our advertisers, including the directory participants, as those links alone now are driving substantial traffic to our customers.

The one-two combination of the graphical directory listing on <http://www.violinist.com/shop> and the text link on all other pages of the website made the package we were selling a great value for violin-related businesses. That made mobilizing to action by selling the packages easy, as many customers were eager to take this opportunity to get their message on a site that many of them either couldn't afford or hadn't considered before. As a result, we were able to implement the feature in 2011 with several thousand dollars of new annual sponsorships for the website. All for creating a simple, flat-file HTML page, a list of text links, and a new link on our navigation bar.

And, finally, once we ran the numbers on clicks and reported those back to our customers, we were able to win renewals and maintain that sponsorship income for a second year.

Stories from a Theme Park Insider

I've written much in this book about your customers' needs. But you have a need, too: a need to make money. If you didn't, you probably wouldn't be working to launch a business. I wrote in Chapter 3 about the three forms of revenue for a publishing business — advertising, grants and direct payments — but most of what I've written about revenue after that has focused on advertising income.

Yet a strong business rests on multiple revenue streams — and that includes not just income from multiple advertisers, but earning additional forms of income as well. Traditionally, publishers have relied upon direct payments in addition to advertising income to support their businesses.

In newspapers, publishers have earned direct payment income through home delivery subscriptions as well as newsrack and over-the-counter sales of single copies. I worked for more than a decade in the newspaper business, speaking frequently with publishers and other business executives who knew every detail of their organizations' budgets. And I learned from them that the money newspapers made from direct sales barely covered the cost of printing and distributing the papers. All the money that paid for the actual reporting, writing and editorial production of the newspaper came from advertising.

Remember that next time a newspaper executive talks about the need for readers to pay for their news online, the way that they'd traditionally paid for it in print. Online delivery slashed the costs of delivering the news. Maintaining Web servers costs so little compared with building, running and stocking a printing plant that it might as well be zero. Newspapers didn't cripple their businesses by giving away stories for free online. They killed themselves by *giving their ads away for free* online for nearly a decade. From the mid-1990s on, many newspapers bundled free online ads with the print ad packages they sold, effectively pricing online advertising at zero. Since advertisers weren't paying for the online ads, and newspapers weren't making any money from them, no one had any incentive to find a way to ensure that online ads *actually worked* — that they drove readers' attention to their advertisers. Those mistakes continue to haunt the online publishing business today, as traditional news publishers struggle to sell effective ads that can earn enough money to support their newsrooms.

That's led many print publications to try to install "paywalls" — forcing their online readers to pay to read stories online, to earn more money for the publication. A few publications, including the *Wall Street Journal* and *Cooks Illustrated*, have had success with "hard" paywalls, where readers must pay to read more than a token amount of content. A few others, such as the New York Times, have earned significant revenue from "soft" paywalls, which allow you to read a certain number of articles per month on direct visits to the website, as well as an unlimited number of articles when you follow links from other sources, such as Twitter, Google or other websites. But many, many other newspapers collectively have poured millions of dollars into developing and marketing online subscription schemes, only to earn pennies on each dollar spent in return.

You simply can't afford to overlook your community's needs when developing your revenue plan. It should be clear to any publisher willing to pay attention that consumers simply aren't willing to pay substantial amounts of money to read "commodity" news online — information that they can get easily for free from other sources, including directly from their local government, schools, area businesses or other news publications. So long as one publisher can find a way to make the advertising and donations numbers work to allow readers to get the news for free, it will remain impossible for other publishers to make significant amounts of money charging for access to the same stories.

That doesn't mean readers won't pay for content that's

delivered online. In fact, the market for electronic stories is *booming* — with consumers now spending billions of dollars a year. But readers aren't paying to read short news items on the Web. They're paying for... eBooks.

A few years ago, I started a weekly feature on ThemeParkInsider.com where I shared a story about something that happened to me when I worked at Walt Disney World's Magic Kingdom. Each week I wrote up a different story, and most weeks, a few readers who'd also worked in theme parks responded in the comments with similar stories of their own.

The feature soon became the most popular on the site, and many readers started posting my stories to other websites. Clearly, my readers wanted more stories about working in the parks, and readers at other websites wanted them, as well. That's when I decided to republish my stories as an eBook.

Let's be clear about the types of content that work well as an eBook. You're looking for:

- epic narratives
- fun collections of engaging vignettes, interviews, or columns
- collections of useful tips, advice, and strategies

...in other words, collections of information that have value for readers — ideally, timeless value. Don't repackage a bunch of random blog posts or daily news stories and expect them to sell. You need to offer something that your readers will be more willing to buy than all those other books available online in eBook stores.

Think about the books you buy and ask yourself: Would I be willing to buy this book if I didn't work for this publication? If you can't answer "yes," move on to another book idea.

The three major eBook retailers allow authors to sell eBooks through them directly, without having to work through an established publisher. Here are the webpages to learn more about eBook publishing through each retailer and to sign up for its program:

- Amazon's Kindle Direct Publishing
  <http://kdp.amazon.com>
- Apple's iBookstore
  <http://www.apple.com/itunes/sellcontent>
- Barnes and Noble's PubIt!
  <http://pubit.barnesandnoble.com>

In addition, you can publish print versions of your books for sale on Amazon and other bookstores through Amazon's print-on-demand publisher, Createspace <https://www.createspace.com>. I'd recommend creating a print version at the same time that you publish an eBook. You'll pick up some additional sales to readers without eBook devices, but a print version can help drive eBook sales, too. If you've got a higher-priced print version of the same title, Amazon will display your eBook price as a "discount" from the higher print price, making the eBook version look like an even better deal and encouraging more sales.

You won't have enough content for a successful eBook when you launch your site, so I'm including this information only to get you thinking about how eBooks might help grow your business in the years ahead, so that you can start developing eBook-appropriate content now. EBooks can help provide a new revenue source to fund the long-form, investigative journalism that's too often cut first when newsroom budgets shrink. In my time working at the *Los Angeles Times*, I saw several of the paper's major reporting projects become print books. With the much lower costs for creating and distributing eBooks, publishers should plan to sell *every* major reporting project they publish as an eBook.

Most newspapers will rush a print book about a local sports team that wins a major championship. But hard-core fans will buy anything associated with their favorite teams. There's no need to wait for a championship season to crank out a "season in review" eBook for every team with a major following that you cover, if you'll be covering sports in your publication. If you'll be covering a geographic community that welcomes a lot of tourists, you absolutely should be producing an eBook guide to your local community as well. Include a local business directory, advice for visitors, and some engaging stories about the local community and its colorful personalities — tales that will entice your far-flung readers to visit.

(By the way, if you're still working for a legacy newspaper or magazine, someone at your publication should be mining your archives for great old stories that could be edited into eBooks. That's a good source of additional revenue that almost all newspapers are ignoring, to their detriment. "True crime" writers have been ripping off newspaper archives for years. There's no good reason why newspapers themselves shouldn't be getting some of that action.)

Publishing a website gives you a huge advantage over other publishers and independent authors selling eBooks: You already will have built an audience of loyal readers. They'll be your action team, providing the initial sales that can help your books make a strong debut on retailers' category bestseller lists (essential for getting your book seen and suggested to more readers). Their reviews of your book on Amazon, Goodreads and other online communities for readers will help spread word about your book at no cost to you — a viral launch that traditional print publishers would have to drop big money on to get for a new author.

So what's your action plan to proceed, once you have the right content in hand? What do you have to do to produce an eBook? Here's the best part — the news that actually made me laugh when I discovered it. You know what an eBook is, from a technical perspective? (You're gonna love this.)

An eBook is essentially... *an HTML document.*

Technically, an eBook is based on XML [Extensible Markup Language], a broader markup language than HTML. But if you've published content in HTML format, you've got the core of an eBook. The .epub (eBook) document you will upload to Amazon, Apple or Barnes and Noble for them to sell is essentially a compressed XML document, zipped with graphic images, if you're including those in your eBook. I've included the XML coding that you should include at the top and bottom of your core HTML eBook file on *www.robertniles.com/data.*

That said, I wouldn't just string together a bunch of webpages to build an eBook any more than I would slap a broadcast news story script online and call it a blog post. The Web and eBooks are different media, even if they are both most often built upon the written word, formatted in flavors of HTML. Take time to give your work another edit, reordering your reporting as needed and sharpening your language whenever you can. Create a logical chapter structure. I create a new .html file and use NeoOffice Writer/Web for Mac (it's called OpenOffice on Windows) to edit it when I'm writing an eBook, as it allows me to edit text held in HTML source code without having to mess with the underlying HTML. The HTML that NeoOffice generates when I add new paragraphs to the book is quite clean, too. Apple, especially, is quite picky in demanding complaint HTML code in its eBooks. So if you're using a lot of quirky layout and font markup in your stories themselves (as opposed to imposing that through stylesheets), you might need to clean your code before creating your .html file and compressing it into an .epub document. Also be sure that all of the file names you use, for your initial, unzipped .html document and all of your image files, are legal, too. That means no spaces or other illegal characters in the file names.

You'll also need to purchase an ISBN [International Standard Book Number] for every book you publish — that's the unique code bookstores use to identify each book they sell. In the United States, you buy ISBNs from Bowker <*https://www.myidentifiers.com*>, and there's a huge discount for buying in bulk. You'll need to include the ISBN inside the book, on the copyright page. If you create a print version of your book, you'll need to include the ISBN on the back cover, near the price code, as well. Note that you will need separate ISBNs for the eBook and print versions of the same book.

Your final step before exporting your .html file into .epub format is to create a book cover. Use your graphic design skills — or call upon your action team — to create something you think will elicit clicks when potential buyers see it in thumbnail form on Amazon. (I create all my eBook covers in Pixelmator.) Use a 2-units-wide-by-3-units-tall aspect ratio.

Once you've finished your HTML file with your book copy, your cover image, and any other images that you'll include inside the book, compress them into an .epub file using an eBook creation program, such as Calibre <http://calibre-ebook.com> or eCub <http://www.juliansmart.com/ecub>. Then you're ready to upload to the major online bookstores.

So let's look at the analytics. I launched *Stories from a Theme Park Insider* on Amazon and Apple's iBookstore, blogging about the new book on my website and spreading the word through some of those other websites where people had been posting my stories. That gave my book a strong initial rush of sales, which helped it appear on the travel bestseller lists in both stores. That, in turn, exposed the book to more readers, driving more sales. Within three months, *Stories from a Theme Park Insider* reached #2 on Apple's travel bestsellers list, and the book spent several weeks in the top 10 in travel eBooks on both Apple and Amazon. The book even sold enough copies to crack the top 20 on Amazon's overall travel bestseller list, competing against print volumes. To date, the book has spent more than 300 days in the Top 100 travel books sold on Amazon.com.

In its first year of publication, *Stories from a Theme Park Insider* — a 150-page republication of blog posts and reader comments — generated a five-figure income boost for our publishing company, making it the most successful single product launch in our history. (It's a fun book. Really. I hope you'll make it the next book you read!)

You can make money online — don't listen to anyone who says otherwise

So there you go. You *can* make money online and create great journalism at the same time. You can serve your community, bringing it better and deeper coverage than it ever enjoyed before, and you can make a profit while doing it. The key to making this happen, though, is to forget about yourself and your needs and to focus instead on the needs of your community. If you find a need — and meet it — you'll build an audience. And if you build an audience — money will come looking for you.

Many journalists trying to start their own news websites share a common fear — they're afraid of selling ads. Years of news industry training have taught them that asking for money is bad and that journalists who do anything for advertisers are betraying their craft.

Allow me now to share with you the secret of selling advertising — the way that ethical reporters can sell ads without betraying their readers' trust. (And if you remember my secret about making money, from Chapter 3, this is going to sound very familiar.)

The secret to selling advertising is...

Don't worry about selling ads.

Worry instead about doing all the things I've asked you to do in this book: find a need, reach out to a community, build an audience. Go ahead and make space in your website's design for ads, placed in positions where readers will see them. Create a rate card, price the ads fairly and publish a webpage that tells potential advertisers what you offer, how much it costs and how to place an order.

If you've done all this, truly, and built a well-targeted, large-enough audience of engaged readers that advertisers *need* to reach, you won't have to worry about selling ads. You'll just have to set aside some time to take orders — because the advertisers will come looking for you. Of course, you shouldn't be satisfied with just that income. If you decide that you should to reach out to more potential advertisers to raise even more money for your business (and you should), even then you must remember: *Don't worry about selling ads.*

Don't make the mistake that the newspaper industry did. Your business is not to sell ads. It's to meet your customers' needs. So ask potential advertisers what their needs are. If you think that ads on your site could help meet those needs, tell the people you're speaking with what you offer, whom the ads reach, and how much you charge. Let them make the decision.

If you don't think that your ads will help, for Heaven's sake, don't make the offer. Never take an ad order that you think won't help the advertiser. Collecting money without solving needs provides the surest formula for running a business out of business, and soon. Find another way to meet that need, or find another customer.

Don't worry about selling your editorial integrity. That's not on your rate card and it's not up for sale. (At least, it shouldn't be.) You're not selling your content when you sell an ad — you're selling access to your readers. It's just ad space. It's up to your sponsors to use that space effectively, to make their own connections with your readers. As part of my service to my customers, I share what I've learned from working with other sponsors about what kind of images, designs and offers elicit the most clicks and sales, if an advertiser needs help in creating an ad. But I leave it to them to design the ad files.

Good customers don't want you to change what you're doing

in your publication anyway. They want to be on your website because you are serving and attracting the readers they need to reach. If you stop serving that audience and lose readers, you'll lose those advertisers, no matter what you write (or don't write) about them. Remember, it's not about you. It's about your readers. Period. In everything.

Now that that's out of the way, it's time for your final exercise — to start building your publishing business. Take what you've learned from this book, develop your action team, build on the skills and tools you developed doing the exercises along the way and get going. Use the steps of community organizing to build *your* community of readers and customers online. Engage with that community and use what you learn from them to grow a sustainable business that will continue to serve both that community and your career, for many, many years to come.

And please, stay in touch with me, too. I'd love to hear about your journey. I'd like to invite you to follow me on Twitter *@robertniles*, where I post about publishing issues and entrepreneurship. If you "Like" this book on Facebook, too, I'll share some of the stories of your fellow readers on that page, too. On both services I'll keep you up-to-date on any changes or additions I might make to this book in future editions. If you have suggestions or personal stories you'd like to share in a future edition, drop me a line via *robert@robertniles.com*.

I love online publishing. I love working for myself and working for a community, too. I don't miss the bureaucracy, endless meetings and office politics of corporate publishing one bit. I hope that this book will help guide you toward a successful career in independent online publishing. Your community needs people like you. Don't leave them waiting.

APPENDIX: STATISTICS EVERY WRITER SHOULD KNOW

Numbers can't "talk," but they can tell you as much as your human sources can. But as with human sources, you have to ask!

So what should you ask a number? Well, mathematicians have developed an entire field — statistics — dedicated to getting answers out of numbers. Now, you don't have to have a degree in statistics in order to conduct an effective "interview" with your data. But you do need to know a few basics.

In 1996, I first published an online tutorial for math-phobic journalists, called *Statistics Every Writer Should Know.* I majored in a program called "Mathematical Methods in the Social Sciences" at Northwestern University (try to fit *that* on a job application!), and thought that I could use my math background to help some of my fellow newspaper reporters become less afraid of numbers. The website attracted a lot of attention, and over the years, I've received hundreds of emails from students thanking me for saving their rear end on their statistics finals. That wasn't the audience I was aiming for, but hey, I'm happy to help anyone.

Running a business demands at least a basic knowledge of math and math concepts, so I'm including this tutorial here, as an appendix to the book. I've rewritten and updated several of the sections, so even if you've followed my work online, I hope you'll find this version of the tutorial even more helpful.

Here, described in plain English, are some basic concepts in statistics that every writer should know...

Mean

This is one of the more common statistics you will see. And it's easy to compute. All you have to do is *add* up all the values in a set of data and then *divide* that sum by the number of values in the dataset. Here's an example:

Let's say you are writing about the World Wide Widget Co. and the salaries of its nine employees.

> The CEO makes $100,000 per year,
> Two managers make $50,000 per year,
> Four factory workers make $15,000 each, and
> Two trainees make $9,000 per year.

So you **add** $100,000 + $50,000 + $50,000 + $15,000 + $15,000 + $15,000 + $15,000 + $9,000 + $9,000 (all the values in the set of data), which gives you $278,000. Then *divide* that total by 9 (the number of values in the set of data).

That gives you the *mean*, which is $30,889.

Not a bad average salary. But be careful when using this number. After all, only three of the nine workers at WWW Co. make that much money. And the other six workers don't even make half the average salary.

So what statistic should you use when you want to give some idea of what the average *worker* at WWW Co. is earning? It's time to learn about the *median*.

Median

Whenever you find yourself writing the words, "the average worker" this, or "the average household" that, you don't want to use the mean to describe those situations. You want a statistic that tells you something about the worker or the household in the middle. That's the *median*.

Again, this statistic is easy to determine because the median literally **is** the value in the middle. Just line up the values in your set of data, from largest to smallest. The one in the dead-center is your median.

For the World Wide Widget Co., here are the workers' salaries:

$100,000
$50,000
$50,000
$15,000
$15,000
$15,000
$15,000
$9,000
$9,000

That's 9 employees. So the one halfway down the list, the fifth value, is $15,000. That's the median. (If you have an even number of values lined up, split the difference between the two in the middle.)

Comparing the mean to the median for a set of data can give you an idea how widely the values in your dataset are spread apart. In this case, there's a somewhat substantial gap between the CEO at WWW Co. and the rank and file. Of course, in the real world, a set of just nine numbers won't be enough to tell you very much about anything. But we're using a small dataset here to help keep these concepts clear.

Here's another illustration of this concept. Ten people are riding on a bus in Redmond, Washington. The mean income of those riders is $50,000 a year. The median income of those riders is also $50,000 a year.

Joe Bleaux gets off the bus. Bill Gates gets on.

The median income of those riders remains $50,000 a year. But the mean income is now somewhere in the neighborhood of several million dollars or so. A clueless or dishonest reporter could jump in now to say that the average income of those bus riders is several million bucks. But those other nine riders didn't become millionaires just because Bill Gates got on their bus. A reporter who writes that the "average rider" on that bus earns $50,000 a year, using the median instead of the mean, provides a far more accurate picture of those bus riders' place in the economy.

Statisticians have a value, called a *standard deviation* [SD], that tells them how widely the values in a set are spread apart. A large SD tells you that the data are fairly diverse, while a small SD tells you the data are pretty tightly bunched together. If you'll be doing a lot of work with numbers or scientific research, it will be worth your time to learn a bit about the standard deviation. We'll get to that definition in a bit.

If you are interested, I'll tell you the definition of the *mode*, too.

Mode

The mode is the value in a set that occurs the most often. That's it.

Pretty easy, huh? No math here, no need to drag out the calculator. Just count 'em up, and whoever has the most tally marks wins. That's the mode.

So when would you use this in a story? Almost never.

Sorry about that. Yeah, I know, it stinks — the easier the math, the less useful it is to you. But there are times when you can slip the mode into a story. Let's say you were writing about Halloween costumes, for example. Wouldn't it be nice to include which costume was the most popular at a given store, or something like that?

That's when you would use the mode in a story — as the most popular example from a list of... whatever. (Halloween costumes sold in a store, candy brands collected trick or treating, brands of toilet paper used to TP houses, etc.)

So, to wrap this up, here's when you would use the median, the mean and the mode in a news story.

Use the median to describe how much money the typical customer spent at a Halloween costume shop.

Use the mean to describe how much money the Halloween costume shop collected per customer this season. (This number usually will be larger than the median, because it is skewed upward by a few big customers — rich guys who want to dress up their whole office like the cast of "Star Wars" or something equally outlandish.)

Use the mode to describe what was the most popular single

costume sold at the shop this season.

I hope that wasn't too scary.

Percent Change

Percent changes are useful to help people understand changes in a value over time. Again, figuring this one requires nothing more than fourth-grade math.

Simply *subtract* the old value from the new value, then *divide* by the old value.

Multiply the result by 100 and slap a % sign on it. That's your percent change.

Let's say Springfield had 50 murders last year, as did Capital City. So there's no difference in crime between these cities, right? Maybe, maybe not. Let's go back and look at the number of murders in those towns in previous years, so we can determine a percent change.

Five years ago, Capital City had 42 murders while Springfield had just 29.

Subtract the old value from the new one for each city and then divide by the old values. For Capital City that means taking 50-42 and dividing that result by 42. For Springfield, figure 50-29 and divide that result by 29. That will show you that, over a five year period, Capital City had a 19 percent increase in murders, while Springfield's increase was more than 72 percent.

That's your lead.

Or is it? There's something else to consider when computing percent change. Take a look at a concept called *per capita* to find out.

Per Capita, Rates and Comparisons

Percent change in a value tells you only part of the story when you are comparing values for several communities or groups. Another important statistic is each group's *per capita* value. This figure helps you compare values among groups of different size.

Let's look at Springfield and Capital City again. This year, 800,000 people live in Springfield while 600,000 live in Capital City. Five years ago, however, just 450,000 people lived in Springfield while 550,000 lived in Capital City.

Why is this important? The fact that Springfield grew so much more than Capital City over the past five years could help explain why the number of murders in Springfield increased by so much over the same period. After all, if there are more people in a city, one might expect there to be more murders.

To find out if one city really is more dangerous than another, you need to determine a *per capita* murder rate. That is, the number of murders *for each person in town*. (That's what "*per capita*" means. It's Latin for "for each unit.")

To find that rate, simply *divide* the number of murders by the total population of the city. To keep from using a tiny little decimal, statisticians usually multiply the result by 100,000 and give the result as the number of murders per 100,000 people.

In Springfield's case, 50 murders divided by 800,000 people equals a murder rate of 6.25 per 100,000 people. Capital City's 50 murders divided by 600,000 people equals a murder rate of 8.33 per 100,000 people.

Five years ago, Springfield's 29 murders divided by 450,000 people equaled a murder rate of 6.44 per 100,000 people. And Capital City's 42 murders divided by 550,000 equaled a murder rate of 7.64 per 100,000 people.

In the previous section, we found that the number of murders in Springfield increased 72 percent over five years, while the number of murders in Capital City grew by just 19 percent. But when we now compare *per capita* murders, Springfield's murder rate decreased by almost 3 percent, while Capital City's per capita murder rate increased by more than 9 percent.

There's the real story.

Remember in Chapter 6, when I wrote about school test scores? That's another example of how reporters can miss stories when they don't make apples-to-apples comparisons with data. It's just not fair to call schools serving poor students "failures" compared to schools with mostly wealthy families, when family poverty is the number-one factor affecting test scores. You've got to account for family income when comparing student test scores across schools and districts. In the same spirit, figuring crime stats, economic data and other community characteristics as *per capita* numbers, instead of using the raw numbers of incidents, can help you make the apples-to-apples comparisons that allow you to report truthful information to your readers.

Standard Deviation

I'll be honest. Standard deviation is a more difficult concept than the others we've covered. And unless you are writing for a specialized, professional audience, you'll probably never use the words "standard deviation" in a story. But that doesn't mean you should ignore this concept.

The standard deviation is kind of the "mean of the mean," and often can help you find the story behind the data. To understand this concept, it can help to learn about what statisticians call "normal distribution" of data.

A normal distribution of data means that most of the examples in a set of data are close to the "average," while relatively few examples tend to one extreme or the other.

Let's say you are writing a story about nutrition. You need to look at people's typical daily calorie consumption. Like most data, the numbers for people's typical consumption probably will turn out to be normally distributed. That is, for most people, their consumption will be close to the mean, while fewer people eat a lot more or a lot less than the mean.

When you think about it, that's just common sense. Not that many people are getting by on a single serving of kelp and rice. Or on eight meals of steak and milkshakes. Most people lie somewhere in between.

If you looked at normally distributed data on a graph, it would look something like this:

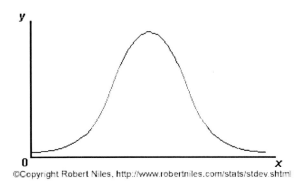

The **x**-axis (the horizontal one) is the value in question... calories consumed, dollars earned or crimes committed, for example. And the **y**-axis (the vertical one) is the number of datapoints for each value on the **x**-axis... in other words, the number of people who eat **x** calories, the number of households that earn **x** dollars, or the number of cities with **x** crimes committed.

Now, not all sets of data will have graphs that look this perfect. Some will have relatively flat curves, others will be pretty steep. Sometimes the mean will lean a little bit to one side or the other. But all normally distributed data will have something like this same "bell curve" shape.

The **standard deviation** is a statistic that tells you how tightly all the various examples are clustered around the mean in a set of data. When the examples are pretty tightly bunched together and the bell-shaped curve is steep, the standard deviation is small. When the examples are spread apart and the bell curve is relatively flat, that tells you you have a relatively large standard deviation.

Computing the value of a standard deviation is complicated. But let me show you graphically what a standard deviation represents...

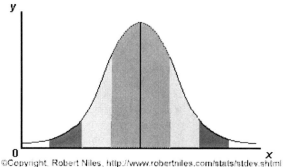

One standard deviation away from the mean in either direction on the horizontal axis (the two shaded areas closest to the center axis on the above graph) accounts for somewhere around 68 percent of the people in this group. Two standard deviations away from the mean (the four areas closest to the center areas) account for roughly 95 percent of the people. And three standard deviations (all the shaded areas) account for about 99 percent of the people.

If this curve were flatter and more spread out, the standard deviation would have to be larger in order to account for those 68 percent or so of the people. So that's why the standard deviation can tell you how spread out the examples in a set are from the mean.

Why is this useful? Here's an example: If you are comparing test scores for different schools, the standard deviation will tell you how diverse the test scores are for each school.

Let's say Springfield Elementary has a higher mean test score than Shelbyville Elementary. Your first reaction might be to say that the kids at Springfield are smarter.

But a bigger standard deviation for one school tells you that there are relatively more kids at that school scoring toward one extreme or the other. By asking a few follow-up questions you might find that, say, Springfield's mean was skewed up because the school district sends all of the gifted education kids to Springfield. Or that Shelbyville's scores were dragged down because students who recently have been "mainstreamed" from special education classes have all been sent to Shelbyville.

In this way, looking at the standard deviation can help point you in the right direction when asking why information is the way it is.

The standard deviation can also help you evaluate the worth of all those so-called "studies" that seem to be released to the press everyday. A large standard deviation in a study that claims to show a relationship between eating Twinkies and shooting politicians, for example, might tip you off that the study's claims aren't all that trustworthy.

Of course, you'll want to seek the advice of a trained statistician whenever you try to evaluate the worth of any scientific research. But if you know at least a little about standard deviation going in, that will make your talk with him or her much more productive.

Okay, because so many of you asked nicely...
Here is *one* formula for computing the standard deviation. A warning, this is for **math geeks only!** Writers and others seeking only a basic understanding of stats don't need to read any more in this chapter. Remember, a decent calculator or a stats program will calculate this for you...

Terms you'll need to know
x = one value in your set of data
avg (x) = the mean (average) of all values x in your set of data
n = the number of values x in your set of data

For each value x, subtract the overall avg (x) from x, then multiply that result by itself (otherwise known as determining the square of that value). Sum up all those squared values. Then divide **that** result by (n-1). Got it? Then, there's one more step... find the square root of that last number. *That's* the standard deviation of your set of data.

Now, remember how I told you this was *one* way of computing this? Sometimes, you divide by (n) instead of (n-1). It's too complex to explain here. So don't try to go figuring out a standard deviation if you just learned about it on this page. Just be satisfied that you've now got a grasp on the basic concept.

The more practical way to compute it...
In Microsoft Excel, type the following code into the cell where you want the Standard Deviation result, using the "unbiased," or "n-1" method:

=STDEV(A1:Z99) *(substitute the cell name of the first value in your dataset for A1, and the cell name of the last value for Z99.)*

Or, use...

=STDEVP(A1:Z99) if you want to use the "biased" or "n" method.

Survey Sample Sizes and Margin of Error

The most accurate survey of a group of people is a vote: Just ask everyone to make a decision and tally the ballots. It's 100% accurate, assuming you counted the votes correctly.

(By the way, there's a whole other topic in math that describes the errors people can make when they try to measure things like that. But, for now, let's assume you can count with 100% accuracy.)

Here's the problem: Running elections costs a lot of money. It's simply not practical to conduct a public election every time you want to test a new product or ad campaign. So companies, campaigns and news organizations ask a randomly selected small number of people instead. The idea is that you're surveying a sample of people who will accurately represent the beliefs or opinions of the entire population.

But how many people do you need to ask to get a representative sample?

The best way to figure this one is to think about it backwards. Let's say you picked a specific number of people in the United States at random. What then is the chance that the people you picked *do not* accurately represent the U.S. population as a whole? For example, what is the chance that the percentage of those people you picked who said their favorite color was blue does *not* match the percentage of people in the entire U.S. who like blue best?

Of course, our little mental exercise here assumes you didn't do anything sneaky like phrase your question in a way to make people more or less likely to pick blue as their favorite color. Like, say, telling people "You know, the color blue has been linked to cancer. Now that I've told you that, what is your favorite color?" That's called a leading question, and it's a big no-no in surveying.

Common sense will tell you (if you listen...) that the chance that your sample is off the mark will *decrease* as you add more people to your sample. In other words, the more people you ask, the more likely you are to get a representative sample. This is easy so far, right?

Okay, enough with the common sense. It's time for some math. *(insert smirk here)* The formula that describes the relationship I just mentioned is basically this:

The margin of error in a sample = 1 divided by the square root of the number of people in the sample

How did someone come up with that formula, you ask? Like most formulas in statistics, this one can trace its roots back to pathetic gamblers who were so desperate to hit the jackpot that they'd even stoop to mathematics for an "edge." If you really want to know the gory details, the formula is derived from the standard deviation of the proportion of times that a researcher gets a sample "right," given a whole bunch of samples.

Which is mathematical jargon for..."Trust me. It works, okay?"

So a sample of just 1,600 people gives you a margin of error of 2.5 percent, which is pretty darn good for a poll.

You've probably heard that term — "margin of error" — a lot before. Reporters throw it around like a hot potato — like if they linger with it too long (say, by trying to explain what it means), they'll just get burned. That's because many reporters have no idea what a "margin of error" really represents.

I gave you the math up above. But let's talk about what that math represents. When you do a poll or survey, you're making a very educated guess about what the larger population thinks. If a poll has a margin of error of 2.5 percent, that means that if you ran that poll 100 times — asking a different sample of people each time — the overall percentage of people who responded the same way would remain within 2.5 percent of your original result in at least

95 of those 100 polls.

(WARNING: Math Geek Stuff!)
Why 95 times out of 100? In reality, the margin of error is what statisticians call a **confidence interval**. The math behind it is much like the math behind the standard deviation. So you can think of the margin of error at the 95 percent confidence interval as being equal to two standard deviations in your polling sample. Occasionally you will see surveys with a 99-percent confidence interval, which would correspond to three standard deviations and a much larger margin of error.
(End of Math Geek Stuff!)

If a poll says that 48 percent of registered voters surveyed are likely to vote for Candidate A and 46 precent of those voters plan to cast their ballots for Candidate B, you'll likely hear reporters saying that Candidate A has a two-point lead. Now that's true *in this poll*, but given the likely margin of error, a mathematician wouldn't say that Candidate A has a two-point lead in the actual race. There's just too much of a chance that Candidate A's true support is enough less than 48 percent and the Candidate B's true support is enough higher than 46 percent that the two might actually be tied, or maybe even that Candidate B might have a slight lead. You can't say for sure on the basis of a single poll with a two-point gap.

If you want to get a more accurate picture of who's going to win the election, you need to look at more polls. Just as asking more people in one poll helps reduce your margin of error, looking at multiple polls can help you get a more accurate view of what people really think. Analysts such as Nate Silver <http://fivethirtyeight.blogs.nytimes.com> and Sam Wang <http://election.princeton.edu> have created models that average multiple polls to help predict which candidates are most likely to win elections. (Silver got his start using baseball statistics to predict future on-field performance, which goes to show that numbers can help you predict things other than elections.) In 2012, Silver was 50-for-50 in predicting state results in the presidential election, based on his model for averaging publicly available polls.

Now, remember that the size of the entire population doesn't matter when you're measuring the accuracy of polls. You could have a nation of 250,000 people or 250 million and that won't affect how big your sample needs to be to come within your desired margin of error. The Math Gods just don't care.

Sometimes you'll see polls with anywhere from 600 to 1,800 people, all promising the same margin of error. That's because pollsters often want to break down their poll results by the gender, age, race or income of the people in the sample. To do that, the pollster needs to have enough women, for example, in the overall sample to ensure a reasonable margin or error among just the women. And the same goes for young adults, retirees, rich people, poor people, etc. That means that in order to have a poll with a margin of error of five percent among many different subgroups, a survey will need to include many more than the minimum 400 people to get that five percent margin in the overall sample.

Regression Analysis

Statisticians are always looking for formulas to describe relationships. But instead of using relationship formulas that we're all familiar with, such as "the rebound", "the gold-digger" and the "friends with benefits," statisticians just use... math.

The simplest type of *math* formula you can use to describe a relationship is just a straight line. We geeks call that a "linear relationship." (Linear = line, get it?) I bet you've heard a lot of sayings that describe a linear relationship:

"The more you put into something, the more you'll get out."

Or, alternately, "Garbage in, garbage out."

Or, the Hollywood version: "Stupid is as stupid does."

But here's what a linear relationship looks like on a graph:

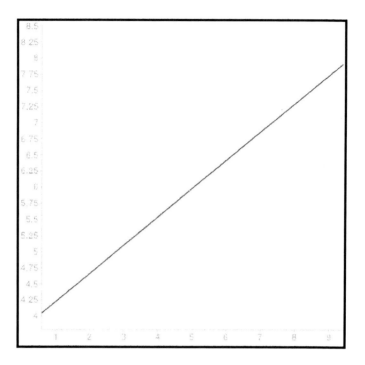

So as the value along the bottom (x) increases, the value along the side (y) gets bigger, too.

How does that line describe a relationship? Well, let's try this:

The more I work out at the gym, the more likely people at this bar are going to find me attractive.

Or, for you cynics out there:

The more I drink at this bar, the more likely I am to find these other people attractive.

Okay, you get the idea.

Generalizations such as these might be nice to know, but a statistician wants to get specific. She wants to know *exactly* how many more push-ups a person has to do to elicit an extra glance.

Or how many beers your friend has to drink before he agrees to audition for a reality-TV dating show.

Statisticians are number geeks, remember?

More importantly, they want to test to see if the generalization is actually true. So they collect data — in other words, they go out and write down information. Maybe you track the number of dates someone gets each week after he starts a work-out program. Or you sit back and record the number of people a drunk hits on in a bar, along with the number of drinks he consumes.

Whatever you're studying, you want to collect two variables of information — an *independent variable* (for example: whatever thing you do first, such as weeks working out or beers consumed), and the *dependent variable* (the other thing that we think might result from doing the first thing, such as the number of dates you get or the number of failed passes you make).

Once you've collected your data, it's time to plot the numbers on a graph, like this:

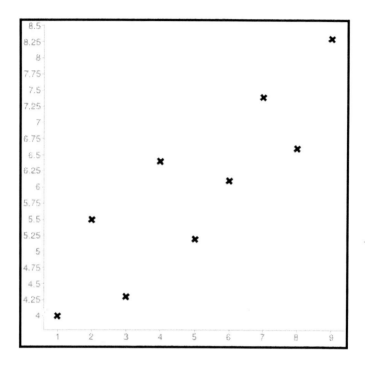

Okay, I can imagine you shaking your head. "But these points don't make a straight line!" you're thinking to yourself. Right?

Well, you are right.

Trying to connect these dots might form some weird shape, but it won't be the nice, smooth straight line that a statistician needs to describe a linear relationship. So we do the next best thing — we try to draw the line that comes as close as we can to as many of these data points as possible.

And, yep, statisticians have created a math formula to do just that. They call this formula "least squares regression."

Why that clumsy name?

Actually, the name isn't clumsy at all. It describes exactly what this equation does. A least squares regression finds the line that comes closest to the data points on the graph. Why "least squares"? Imagine you drew a square for each data point on the graph. The data point itself would be one corner of the square and the point where the square meets the line would be on another corner. The position of the line that minimizes the size of all those squares added together is the least squares regression line. (You can find an online widget to plot least-squares regression lines at <*http://www.alcula.com/calculators/statistics/linear-regression*>.)

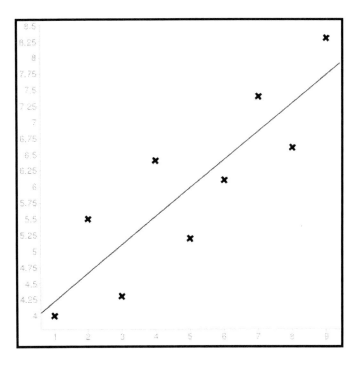

Why use squares? Why not just draw a bunch of other lines, connecting the data points with the line you're trying to draw? Here's the problem with that: Some data points lie above the line, and others lie below it. If you just measured distances away from the line, you'd have positive numbers from the data points above the line, and negative numbers for the data points below the line. But you don't want those numbers to cancel each other out. You want to add the absolute values of all those numbers instead.

Rather than do that, if you just square all those distances, you get positive values for them all anyway. That's a lot simpler for mathematicians to express in an equation. Plus, using squares really penalizes lines that get too far from some of their data points, allowing you to find a line with a much more precise fit to your data.

The exact precision of that fit is measured by a result called R^2 (R-squared). That number, measured between 0 and 1, tells you how much of the variation in the dependent variable is explained by the independent variable. One is a perfect fit. Zero — not so much. (The rest, figured by one minus the R^2 value, is how much of the variation in the dependent variable is explained by error.)

Statisticians have a process called **ANOVA (Analysis of Variance)**, which generates R^2 and a whole bunch of numbers that can tell you whether your least squares regression line expresses a "statistically significant" relationship... or if you've just been drinking too much and your numbers don't mean a thing.

Remember, a regression analysis only tells you how well two variables are correlated with one another. But correlation *does not* imply causation. Here's an example: A study might find that an increase in the local birth rate was correlated with the annual migration of storks over the town. This does not mean that the storks brought the babies. Or that the babies brought the storks.

Statisticians call this sort of thing a "spurious correlation," which is a fancy term for "total coincidence."

People who want something from others often use regression studies to try to support their cause. They'll say something along the lines of "a study shows that a new police policy that we want led to a 20 percent drop in crime over a 10-year period in (some city)."

That might be true, but the drop in crime could be due to something other than that new policy. What if, say, the average age of those cities' residents increased significantly over that 10 year period? Since crime is believed to be age-dependent (meaning the more young men you have in an area, the more crime you have), the aging of the population could potentially be the cause of the drop in crime.

The policy change and the drop in crime might have been correlated. But that does not mean that one caused the other.

Data Analysis

You wouldn't buy a car or a house without asking some questions about it first. So don't go buying into someone else's data without asking questions, either.

Okay, you're saying... but with data there are no tires to kick, no doors to slam, no basement walls to check for water damage. Just numbers, graphs and other scary statistical things that are causing you to have bad flashbacks to your last income tax return. What the heck can you ask about data?

Plenty. Here are a few standard questions you should ask any human beings who slap a pile of data in front of you and ask you write about it.

Where did the data come from?

Always ask this one first. You always want to know who did the research that created the data you're going to write about.

You'd be surprised — sometimes it turns out that the person who is feeding you a bunch of numbers can't tell you where they came from. That should be your first hint that you need to be very skeptical about what you are being told.

Even if your data have an identifiable source, you still want to know what it is. You might have some extra questions about a medical study on the effects of secondhand smoking if you were to learn that it came from researchers employed by a tobacco company instead of from, say, a team of research physicians from a major medical school. You might question a study about water safety that came from a political interest group that had been lobbying Congress for a ban on pesticides.

Just because a report comes from a group with a vested interest in its results doesn't guarantee the report is a sham. But you should always be skeptical when looking at research generated by people with a political agenda. At the very least, they have plenty of incentive NOT to tell you about data they found that contradict their organization's position.

Which brings us to the next question:

Have the data been peer-reviewed?

Major studies that appear in journals like the *New England Journal of Medicine* undergo a process called "peer review" before they are published. That means that professionals — doctors, statisticians, etc. — have looked at the study before it was published and concluded that the study's authors followed the rules of good scientific research and didn't torture their data like a middle ages infidel to make the numbers conform to their conclusions.

Always ask if research was formally peer reviewed. If it was, you know that the data you'll be looking at are at least minimally reliable.

And if it wasn't peer-reviewed, ask why. It might be that the research just wasn't interesting to enough people to warrant peer review. Or it could mean that the research had as much chance of standing up to professional scrutiny as a $500 mobile home has of standing up in a tornado.

How were the data collected?

This one is real important to ask, especially if the data were not peer-reviewed. If the data come from a survey, for example, you want to know that the people who responded to the survey were selected at random.

How many times have you seen news reports based on call-in polls or website surveys? Those can be fun (see my notes on the ladder of engagement in Chapter 8), but they aren't news that other publications should be reporting. Why? These types of surveys simply reflect the views of what statisticians call a "self-selected sample." People who feel really passionately about one side or the other can flood the poll, skewing the results from what they would have been had you polled only a random sample of people in the community. When this happens in online surveys, it's called "Freeping" the poll, after the website FreeRepublic.com, whose readers have become notorious over the years for doing this sort of thing to polls on other websites.

Another problem with data is "cherry-picking." This is the social-science equivalent of gerrymandering, where you draw up a legislative district so that all the people who are going to vote for your candidate are included in your district and everyone else is scattered among a bunch of other districts.

Be on the lookout for cherry-picking, for example, in epidemiological (*a fancy word for the study of disease that sometimes means: "We didn't go out and collect any data ourselves. We just used someone else's data and played 'connect the dots' with them in an attempt to find something interesting"*) studies looking at illnesses in areas surrounding toxic-waste dumps, power lines, high school cafeterias, etc. It is all too easy for a lazy researcher to draw the boundaries of the area he or she is looking at to include several extra cases of the illness in question and exclude many healthy individuals in the same area.

When in doubt, plot the subjects of a study on map and look for yourself to see if the boundaries make sense.

Finally, be aware of numbers taken out of context.

Again, data that are "cherry picked" to look interesting might mean something else entirely once they are placed in a different context.

Consider the following example from Eric Meyer, a professional reporter who went on to teach the University of Illinois:

"My personal favorite was a habit we use to have years ago, when I was working in Milwaukee. Whenever it snowed heavily, we'd call the sheriff's office, which was responsible for patrolling the freeways, and ask how many fender-benders had been reported that day. Inevitably, we'd have a lede that said something like, "A fierce winter storm dumped 8 inches of snow on Milwaukee, snarled rush-hour traffic and caused 28 fender-benders on county freeways" — until one day I dared to ask the sheriff's department how many fender-benders were reported on clear, sunny days. The answer — 48 — made me wonder whether in the future we'd run stories saying, "A fierce winter snowstorm prevented 20 fender-benders on county freeways today." There may or may not have been more accidents per mile traveled in the snow, but clearly there were fewer accidents when it snowed than when it did not."

It is easy for people to go into brain-lock when they see a stack of papers loaded with numbers, spreadsheets and graphs. (And some sleazy sources are counting on it.) But your readers are depending upon you to make sense of that data for them.

Use what you've learned on this page to look at data with a more critical attitude. (That's critical, not cynical. There is a great deal of excellent data out there.) The worst thing you can do as a writer is to pass along someone else's word about data without having any idea whether that person's worth believing or not.

Picking the Right Statistical Test

Congratulations! Most journalists have no clue that there *are* different tests for different situations.

Here's the best advice I can give you: Talk to a pro. You know how great copy editors can catch errors in syntax, usage and vocabulary that even experienced writers rarely notice? Professional statisticians do the same thing with numbers.

Smart reporters run their words by a copy editor before they hit print. Why not run your data past a statistician before publishing them?

Unfortunately, I don't know of many publications that have people with statistics degrees on their editorial staff. While managers might not feel that correct numbers and proper analysis are important, our readers do. And the screw-ups that our collective lack of attention to things like statistics has caused might be part of the reason why readership's dropping at so many U.S. newspapers.

Call the press relations department of your local college or university and ask for a contact in the statistics department. Then talk with that source about what you have and what you want to do. As with any source, it's best to establish the relationship *off deadline*, when you have time to ask questions and wait for thoughtful answers.

"Okay, that's nice, Robert," you say. "Um, I'm under deadline now for this story/article/paper/homework assignment, and really need to know what to do...." Well, then, here are some tips:

The best resource I've found for figuring out the right test to run is Selecting Statistics <*http://www.socialresearchmethods.net/selstat/ssstart.htm*>, from Bill Trochim at Cornell University. To use this site, you'll need to know a little bit about your data. The site will ask you a series of questions about your data, and pick the right test for you, based on your answers.

If you want to understand *why* a specific test is the right choice, try *Intuitive Biostatistics*: Choosing a statistical test <*http://www.graphpad.com/support/faqid/1790*>, an online chapter to a stats textbook.

When you're ready to conduct your test, you'll find links to several nifty web pages that perform stats calculations at statpages.org. And additional information on testing can be found at David Lane's HyperStat Online <*http://davidmlane.com/hyperstat*>.

ABOUT THE AUTHOR

Robert Niles has trained hundreds of journalists in entrepreneurship, both as an adjunct instructor at the University of Southern California's Annenberg School of Journalism and as lead faculty for the Knight Digital Media Center News Entrepreneur Boot Camps. Today, he publishes ThemeParkInsider.com, an online consumers' guide to the world's leading theme and amusement parks, and with his wife, Laurie, publishes Violinist.com, one of the largest and most respected online communities of violin professionals, students and fans.

ThemeParkInsider.com has been named the top theme park site on the Internet by *Forbes* and *Travel + Leisure* magazines, has been a Webby Awards finalist and a winner of the Online Journalism Award, presented by the Online News Association and the Columbia Graduate School of Journalism.

Robert worked at Walt Disney World's Magic Kingdom for five summers between 1987 and 1991, as well as for a full year between graduating Northwestern University and beginning graduate school in journalism at another university. In the years since leaving Disney, Robert has worked as a reporter, editorial writer, columnist and website editor for several newspapers, including *The* [Bloomington, Indiana] *Herald-Times*, the *Omaha* [Nebraska] *World-Herald*, the [Denver] *Rocky Mountain News* and the *Los Angeles Times*.

Robert is a native of Los Angeles and today lives in Pasadena, California with his wife and two children. You can follow Robert on Twitter @robertniles <*http://twitter.com/robertniles*>.

CPSIA information can be obtained at www.ICGtesting.com
Printed in the USA
LVOW10s2001210414

382585LV00014BA/762/P